X
25-

D1615850

BENEATH PEARL HARBOR USS ARIZONA

UNDERWATER VIEWS OF AN AMERICAN ICON

BY BRETT T. SEYMOUR & NAOMI S. BLINICK

IN PARTNERSHIP WITH

THE NATIONAL PARK SERVICE

NPS SUBMERGED RESOURCES CENTER

WORLD WAR II VALOR IN THE PACIFIC NATIONAL MONUMENT

PACIFIC HISTORIC PARKS

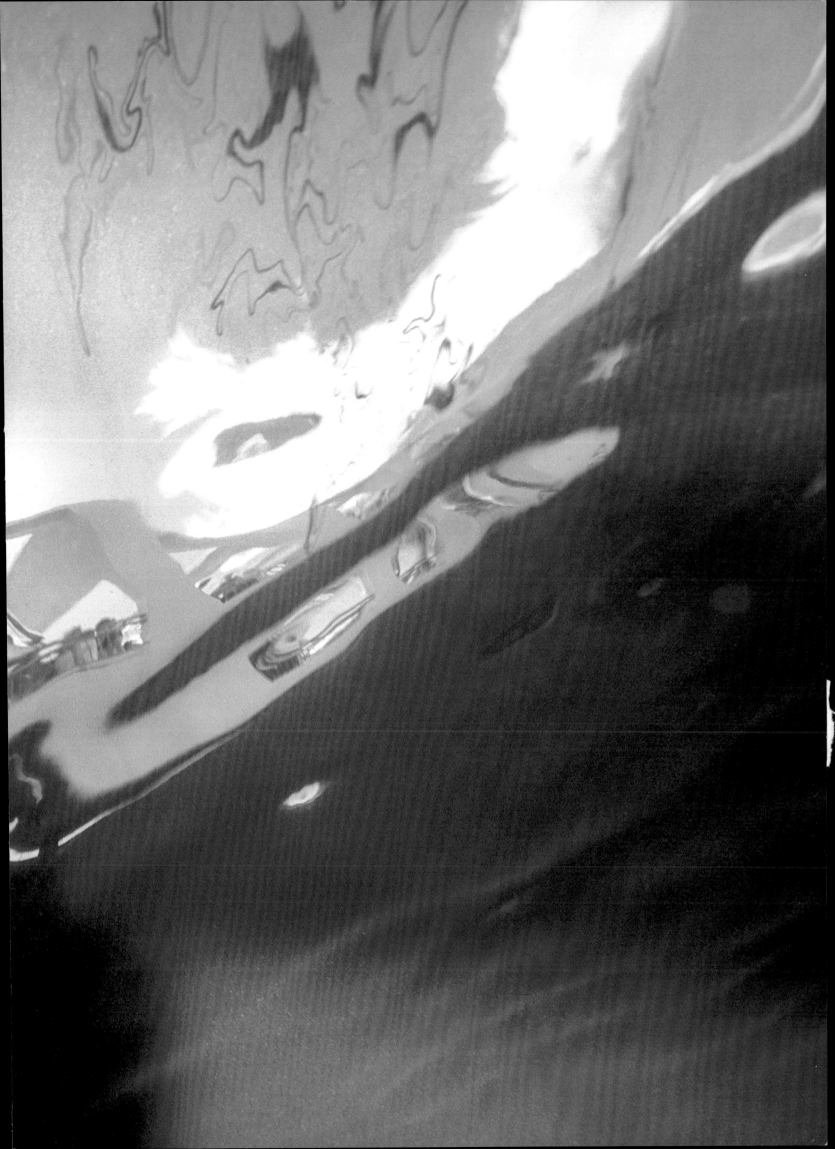

Copyright © 2016 by Best Publishing Company.

All photographs are a work of the United States Government as defined in the Copyright Act (17 U.S.C. §§ 101 and 105) and therefore are in the public domain.

Survivor quotes were obtained from oral history transcripts produced by the National Park Service, the Naval Historical Center, and television station KTEH in Honolulu, HI, and are in the public domain.

ISBN 978-1-930536-98-2
Library of Congress Control Number: 2016954838

Version 1.0

All rights reserved. No part of this book may be reproduced, stored in a retrieval system, or transmitted in any form or by any means electronic, mechanical, photocopying, microfilming, recording, or otherwise without permission from the publisher (or in the case of photocopying in Canada, without a license from Canopy, the Canadian Copyright Licensing Agency).

Printed and bound in Canada.

Best Publishing Company
631 US Highway 1, Suite 307
North Palm Beach, FL 33408

The opinions expressed in this work are those of the authors and do not reflect the opinions of Best Publishing Company or its editors.

The views expressed in this work are those of the individual authors and do not necessarily represent any position, official or otherwise, of the National Park Service or the United States of America.

Information contained in this work has been obtained by Best Publishing Company and the authors from sources believed to be reliable. However, neither Best Publishing Company nor its authors guarantees the accuracy or completeness of any information published herein, and neither Best Publishing Company nor its authors shall be responsible for any errors, omissions, or claims for damages, including exemplary damages, arising out of use, inability to use, or with regard to the accuracy or sufficiency of the information contained in this publication.

Note: The Submerged Resources Center (SRC) of the NPS was known for its first 20 years as the Submerged Cultural Resources Unit (SCRU). References to work done by the SRC from 1980 to 2000 will often be found under the previous name. The SRC has been operating for 36 consecutive years as of this publication.

Diving is an activity that has inherent risks. An individual may experience injury resulting in disability or death. All persons who wish to engage in diving activities must receive professional instruction. The authors, publisher, and any other party associated with production of this book does not accept responsibility for any accident or injury resulting from diving.

Civilian diving on USS *Arizona* or USS *Utah* is strictly prohibited. Pearl Harbor is an active U.S. Navy base and diving is conducted solely for government-approved purposes.

INTRODUCTION

BY JACQUELINE ASHWELL

Superintendent, World War II Valor In the Pacific National Monument

When USS *Arizona* was commissioned by the United States Navy in 1916, no one knew its fate. None knew that it would become an icon. Today, a century after being placed into active service and 75 years after the attack on Pearl Harbor, USS *Arizona* is visited by millions from across the globe. They come to learn about a pivotal moment in world history. Many come to pay their respects to the 1,177 crewmen killed on December 7, 1941, the majority of whom still rest beneath her decks.

Have you ever wondered what it must have been like to serve aboard USS *Arizona*? Or considered what it means to take care of this precious national icon? Have you stood on the USS *Arizona* Memorial and stared into the depths, wondering what lies below? *Beneath Pearl Harbor* will help answer some of these questions. Within its pages, Brett Seymour and Naomi Blinick have brought together an impressive compilation of stunning images and personal recollections, from those who survived the attack to the stewards who now watch over the ship and its crew.

This book is dedicated to the men of USS *Arizona*, BB-39, in memory of their service and their sacrifice. It is also dedicated to the families who lost sons and brothers and husbands. These are debts that cannot be repaid. In preserving USS *Arizona* for as long as she will last, the National Park Service will continue to share their story with the world.

Previous: Oil released from the ship drifts through this underwater view of the Memorial. This perspective reflects 1.8 million visitors annually as they look down on the submerged battleship. Although divers are the subject of countless tourist photos (note the visitor taking a photo), NPS divers strive to work under the gaze of 1,300 people daily without drawing attention to diving operations.

Following: NPS law enforcement ranger Casey Scott enters the water from the floating Memorial dock for his first orientation dive on *Arizona* as a new NPS diver.

CONTENTS

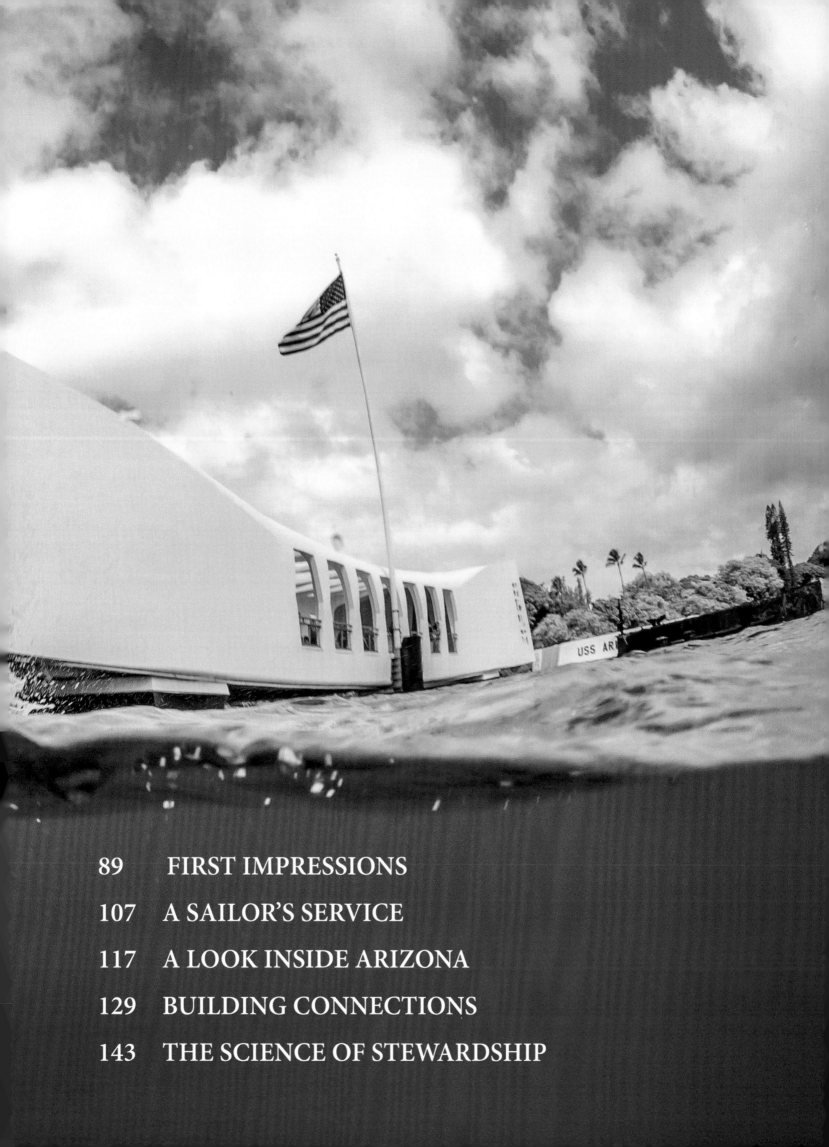

MEMORIAL WALL — U.S.S. ARIZONA

Name	Rank
A. JONES	
W. JONES	Y1c
W. JOYCE	S2c
W. JUDD	F2c
	COX
L. KAGARICE	CSK
O. KAISER	F1c
L. KATT	S2c
D. KELLER	MLDR2c
KELLEY	SF1c
KELLOGG	F1c
KELLY	CEM
KENISTON	
KENISTON	F1c
KENNARD	GM1c
KENNINGTON	S1c
KENNINGTON	
KENT, Jr.	S1c
KIDD	RADM
TLESHIP DIV. COMMANDER	
KIEHN	MM1c
KIESELBACH	CM1c
KING	S1c
KING	S1c
KING	F1c
KING, Jr.	ENS
KINNEY	
KINNEY	QM2c
KIRCHHOFF	
KIRKPATRICK	CAPT
LANN	SC1c
KLINE	GM2c
KLOPP	GM3c
KNIGHT	EM3c
NUBEL, Jr.	
KOCH	S1c
KOENEKAMP	F1c
KOEPPE	SC3c
OLAJACK	S1c
KONNICK	CM2c
KOSEC	BM2c
OVAR	S1c
KRAMB	MSMTH1c
KRAMB	
KRAMER	GM2c
RAUSE	
KRISSMAN	S2c
KRUGER	QM2c
RUPPA	S1c
KUKUK	S1c
LA	SC3c
USIE	RM3c
ADERACH	FC2c
LA FRANCE	S1c
AKE, Jr.	PAYCLK
AKIN	S1c
AKIN	S1c
LA MAR	FC3c
AMB	CSF
NDMAN	
NDRY, Jr.	BKR2c
ANE	COX
ANE	
ANGE	
ANGENWALTER	SK2c
ANOUETTE	COX
ARSON	F3c
A SALLE	
TIN	RM3c
E, Jr.	S1c

Lower left block:
EDY	S1c
GGETT	FC2c
GROS	S1c
IGH	GM3c
OPOLD	ENS
MEISTER	EM3c
	CWT
WIS	CM3c
ISON	FC3c
HTFOOT	GM3c
BO	GM1c

Name	Rank
J. W. LINCOLN	F1c
J. M. LINDSAY	S1c
G. E. LINTON	SF2c
C. W. LIPKE	F2c
J. A. LIPPLE	F2c
D. E. LISENBY	SF1c
R. E. LIVERS	S1c
W. N. LIVERS	S1c
D. A. LOCK	S1c
E. W. LOHMAN	S1c
F. S. LOMAX	ENS
M. LOMBAO	OS1c
B. F. LONG	
T. W. LOUNSBURY	CY
C. B. LOUSTANAU	S1c
F. C. LOVELAND	S1c
N. J. LUCEY	S1c
J. E. LUNA	S1c
E. B. LUZIER	MM2c
E. L. LYNCH	MUS1c
J. R. LYNCH, Jr.	GM2c
W. J. LYNCH, Jr.	
R. D. MADDOX	CEM
A. J. MADRID	S2c
F. R. MAFNAS	MATT2c
G. J. MAGEE	SK3c
F. E. MALECKI	CY
J. S. MALINOWSKI	SM1c
H. L. MALSON	SK1c
E. P. MANION	S2c
A. C. MANLOVE	ELEC
W. E. MANN	GM1c
L. MANNING	S2c
R. F. MANSKE	Y1c
S. M. MARINICH	COX
E. H. MARIS	S1c
J. H. MARLING	S1c
U. H. MARLOW	COX
B. R. MARSH, Jr.	ENS
W. A. MARSH	S1c
T. D. MARSHALL	S1c
H. L. MARTIN	Y1c
J. A. MARTIN	BM1c
J. O. MARTIN	S2c
L. L. MARTIN	F3c
B. D. MASON	S2c
C. H. MASTEL	S1c
D. M. MASTERS	GM3c
C. E. C. MASTERSON	PHM1c
H. R. MATHEIN	BMKR1c
C. H. MATHISON	S1c
V. M. MATNEY	F1c
J. D. MATTOX	AM1c
L. E. MAY	SC2c
G. F. MAYBEE	RM2c
L. E. MAYFIELD	F1c
R. H. MAYO	EM2c
W. M. McCARY	S1c
J. C. McCLAFFERTY	BM2c
H. M. McCLUNG	ENS
L. J. McFADDIN, Jr.	Y2c
J. O. McGLASSON	GM3c
S. W. G. McGRADY	MATT1c
F. R. McGUIRE	SK2c
J. B. McHUGHES	CWT
H. G. McINTOSH	S1c
R. McKINNIE	MATT2c
M. M. McKOSKY	S2c
J. B. McPHERSON	S1c
L. MEANS	MATT1c
J. M. MEARES	S1c
J. A. MENEFEE	S1c

Lower block:
V. G. MENO	MATT2c
S. P. MENZENSKI	COX
H. D. MERRILL	ENS
O. W. MILES	S1c
C. J. MILLER	S1c
	COX
F. N. MILLER	CEM
G. S. MILLER	S1c
J. D. MILLER	S1c
J. Z. MILLER	S1c
W. O. MILLER	SM1c
W. H. MILLIGAN	S1c
R. L. MIMS	S1c

Name	Rank
J. MLINAR	F1c
R. P. MOLPUS	COX
D. MONROE	CMSMTH
R. E. MONTGOMERY	MATT1c
R. E. MOODY	S2c
D. C. MOORE	S1c
F. K. MOORE	S1c
J. C. MOORE	S1c
W. S. MOORHOUSE	SF1c
R. L. MOORMAN	MUS2c
W. MORGAN	S2c
J. O. MORGAREIDGE	F2c
E. E. MORLEY	S1c
O. N. MORRIS	S1c
E. L. MORRISON	S1c
E. C. MORSE	S2c
F. J. MORSE	BM1c
G. R. MORSE	S1c
N. R. MORSE	WT2c
T. L. MOSS	MATT2c
G. E. MOULTON	F1c
C. MUNCY	MM1c
C. L. MURDOCK	WT1c
M. E. MURDOCK	WT2c
J. H. MURPHY	S1c
J. J. MURPHY	S1c
J. P. MURPHY	F1c
T. J. MURPHY, Jr.	SK1c
J. G. MYERS	SK1c
E. H. NAASZ	SF2c
A. J. NADEL	MUS2c
J. G. NATIONS	FC1c
"J" "D" NAYLOR	SM1c
T. D. NEAL	S1c
C. R. NECESSARY	S1c
P. NEIPP	S2c
G. NELSEN	SC2c
H. C. NELSON	S1c
H. C. NELSON	BM1c
L. A. NELSON	S1c
R. E. NELSON	CTC
A. R. NICHOLS	S1c
B. A. NICHOLS	S2c
C. L. NICHOLS	TC1c
J. D. NICHOLS	F1c
G. E. NICHOLSON	EM3c
H. G. NICHOLSON	S1c
T. J. NIDES	EM1c
F. T. NIELSEN	CM1c
R. H. NOONAN	S1c
T. L. NOWOSACKI	ENS
R. A. NUSSER	GM2c
F. E. NYE	S1c
G. D. O'BRYAN	FC1c
J. B. O'BRYAN	FC1c
H. F. OCHOSKI	GM2c
V. S. OFF	S1c
V. W. OGLE	S2c
L. H. OGLESBY	S2c
R. B. OLIVER	S1c
E. K. OLSEN	ENS
G. M. OLSON	S2c
R. E. O'NEALL	S1c
W. T. O'NEILL, Jr.	ENS
D. J. ORR	S1c
S. J. ORZECH	S2c
M. E. OSBORNE	F1c
L. G. OSTRANDER	PHM3c
P. D. OTT	S1c
F. H. OWEN	S2c
R. A. OWENS	SK2c

Lower block:
T. L. OWSLEY	SC1c
A. P. PACE	BM1c
H. ...KES	BM1c
P. J. PAROLI	BKR3c
H. L. PATTERSON	S1c
R. PATTERSON, Jr.	SF1c
H. PAULMAND	OS1c
B. PAVINI	S1c
R. P. PAWLOWSKI	S1c
A. PEARCE, Jr.	S1c
N. C. PEARSON	S2c
R. S. PEARSON	S1c

Name	Rank
H. W. PECKHAM	QM2c
M. V. PEERY	S2c
M. PELESCHAK	S2c
J. A. PELTIER	EM1c
H. L. PENTON	S1c
G. E. PERKINS	F1c
A. H. PETERSON, Jr.	FC1c
E. V. PETERSON	FC2c
H. W. PETERSON	FC1c
R. E. PETERSON	S1c
C. R. PETTIT	CRM
J. J. PETYAK	S1c
G. E. PHELPS	S1c
J. R. PHILBIN	S1c
H. L. PIKE	EM1c
L. J. PIKE	S1c
A. W. PINKHAM	S1c
W. G. PITCHER	GM1c
E. L. POOL	S1c
R. E. POOLE	S1c
D. A. POST	S1c
G. POVESKO	CMM
T. G. POWELL	F1c
W. H. PRESSON	RM1c
A. E. PRICE	S1c
R. L. PRITCHETT, Jr.	S1c
E. L. PUCKETT	SK1c
J. PUGH, Jr.	SF1c
A. B. PUTNAM	S1c
E. PUZIO	S1c
M. J. QUARTO	S1c
J. S. QUINATA	MATT1c
N. J. RADFORD	MUS1c
A. S. RASMUSSEN	CM1c
G. V. RASMUSSON	F1c
W. RATKOVICH	WT1c
G. D. RAWHOUSER	F1c
C. J. RAWSON	BM1c
H. J. RAY	BM1c
C. REAVES	S1c
C. C. RECTOR	SK1c
J. J. REECE	S1c
J. B. REED, Jr.	SK1c
R. E. REED	S2c
P. J. REGISTER	LCDR
J. M. RESTIVO	S1c
E. A. REYNOLDS	S2c
J. F. REYNOLDS	S1c
B. R. RHODES	F2c
M. A. RHODES	S2c
W. A. RICE	S1c
C. E. RICH	S1c
R. L. RICHAR	S1c
W. J. RICHARDSON	COX
F. L. RICHISON	GM1c
A. W. RICHTER	COX
G. A. RICO	S1c
E. E. RIDDELL	S1c
F. RIGANTI	SF1c
G. H. RIGGINS	S1c
F. U. RIVERA	MATT2c
D. F. ROBERTS	F1c
K. F. ROBERTS	BM2c
M. T. ROBERTS	CPHM
W. C. ROBERTS	BKR2c
W. F. ROBERTS	S2c
W. S. ROBERTS, Jr.	RM1c
E. ROBERTSON, Jr.	MATT2c
J. M. ROBERTSON	MM1c
H. T. ROBINSON	S1c
J. J. ROBINSON	EM1c
J. W. ROBINSON	S2c
R. W. ROBINSON	PMH1c
R. A. ROBY	S1c
J. D. RODGERS	S1c
H. T. ROEHM	MM2c
T. S. ROGERS	S1c
S. ROMANO	S1c
D. R. ROMBALSKI	S
V. M. ROMERO	F1c
M. L. ROOT	S1c
C. ...OSE	BM1c
A. ROSENBER	SF1c
D. L. ROSS	S1c
W. F. ROSS	GM1c
E. J. ROWE	S1c
F. M. ROWELL	S2c
W. N. ROYALS	F1c
H. D. ROYER	GM1c
J. F. ROZAR	WT1c
J. S. ROZMUS	OS1c
C. R. RUDDOCK	S1c
W. RUGGERIO	FC1c
R. G. RUNCKEL	BUG1c
N. RUNIAK	S1c
R. P. RUSH	S1c

Name	Rank
O. L. RUSHER	MM1c
J. J. RUSKEY	CBM
J. P. RUTKOWSKI	S1c
D. A. RUTTAN	EM1c
S. R. SAMPSON	RM1c
M. K. SANDALL	SF2c
E. T. SANDERS	S1c
J. H. SANDERSON	ENS
T. S. SANFORD	MUS2c
F. SANTOS	S1c
W. F. SATHER	OC1c
W. S. SAVAGE, Jr.	PMKR1c
T. SAVIN	ENS
M. SAVINSKI	RM1c
J. SCHDOWSKI	S1c
G. A. SCHEUERLEIN	GM1c
E. SCHILLER	S1c
E. P. SCHLUND	MM1c
V. J. SCHMIDT	S1c
H. A. SCHRANK	S1c
H. SCHROEDER	BM1c
H. L. SCHUMAN	SK1c
J. SCHURR	EM1c
H. H. SCILLEY	SF2c
A. J. SCOTT	S1c
J. L. SCRUGGS	MUS2c
R. O. SEAMAN	F1c
W. E. SEELEY	S1c
C. C. SEVIER	S1c
W. A. SHANNON	S1c
H. R. SHARBAUGH	GM1c
L. P. SHARON	MM1c
C. D. SHAW	S1c
R. K. SHAW	MUS1c
G. R. SHEFFER	S1c
W. J. SHERRILL	Y1c
R. S. SHERVEN	EM1c
H. E. SHIFFMAN	RM1c
P. E. SHILKEY	S1c
M. I. SHIMER	S1c
M. H. SHIVE	RM1c
B. F. SHIVELY	F1c
I. SHORES, Jr.	S1c
M. J. SHUGART	S1c
D. D. SIBLEY	S1c
R. L. SIDDERS	S1c
J. H. SIDELL	GM1c
J. SILVEY	MM2c
W. H. SIMON	S1c
A. E. SIMPSON	S1c
H. L. SKEEN	S1c
C. J. SKILES, Jr.	S2c
E. SKILES	S1c
E. C. SLETTO	MM1c
J. G. SMALLEY	S1c
G. D. SMART	COX
H. H. SMESTAD	RM2c
A. J. SMITH	LTJG
E. SMITH	S1c
E. W. SMITH	GM1c
H. SMITH	S1c
J. A. SMITH	SF1c
J. E. SMITH	S1c
L. K. SMITH	S1c
M. L. SMITH	S1c
M. R. SMITH	S1c
O. S. SMITH	S1c
W. T. SMITH	MATT2c
H. M. SOENS	SC1c
J. F. SOOTER	RM1c
H. E. SORENSEN	S1c
C. B. SOUTH	S1c
M. J. SPENCE	S1c
M. E. SPOTZ	F1c
R. L. SPREEMAN	GM2c
C. H. SPRINGER	S1c
K. B. STALLINGS	F1c
...ARKOVICH	S1c
...KOVICH, Jr.	EM1c
...AUDT	F1c
...FFAN	BM2c
...EDER	COX
...HOFF	EM1c
...SON	EM1c
STEVENS	AMM1c
STEWART	SC3c
F. STILLINGS	S1c
W. STOCKMAN	F1c
A. STOCKTON	S
E. STODDARD	S1c
STOPYRA	RM1c
STORM	Y1c
STRANGE	F2c
STRATTON	S1c
SUGGS	S1c

Name	Rank
F. F. SULSER	GM1c
G. A. SUMMERS	S1c
H. E. SUMMERS	Y1c
O. SUMNER	SM2c
C. W. SUTTON	CCSTD
G. W. SUTTON	SK1c
C. E. SWISHER	S1c
H. SYMONETTE	OC1c
V. C. TAMBOLLEO	SF1c
R. A. TANNER	S1c
E. C. TAPIE	GM1c
L. R. TAPP	MM2c
J. TARG	GM1c
A. G. TAYLOR	CWT
C. B. TAYLOR	MATT1c
H. T. TAYLOR	EM1c
R. D. TAYLOR	GM2c
C. M. TEELING	COX
A. R. TEER	CPRTR
R. C. TENNELL	EM1c
J. R. TERRELL	S1c
R. THEILLER	S1c
H. O. THOMAS	COX
R. J. THOMAS	S1c
S. H. THOMAS	S1c
V. D. THOMAS	F1c
C. L. THOMPSON	COX
I. E. THOMPSON	S1c
R. G. THOMPSON	S1c
J. C. THORMAN	S1c
G. H. THORNTON	EM1c
R. R. TINER	F2c
W. E. TISDALE	CWT
T. E. TRIPLETT	S1c
T. TROVATO	S1c
R. E. TUCKER	S1c
E. E. TUNTLAND	COX
J. M. TURNIPSEED	F1c
L. H. TUSSEY	EM1c
R. TYSON	FC1c
A. C. UHRENHOLDT	ENS
R. D. VALENTE	GM1c
G. W. VAN ATTA	MM1c
J. R. VAN HORN	S1c
F. VAN VALKENBURGH	CAPT
COMMANDING OFFICER	
B. VARCHOL	S1c
W. F. VAUGHAN	S1c
G. E. VEEDER	S1c
G. S. VELIA	S1c
A. E. VIEIRA	S1c
W. A. VOJTA	S1c
A. A. VOSTI	S1c
M. J. WAGNER	
S. A. W...	
B. W...	
H. ...	
I. A. WE...	
D. V. WES...	
F. E. WES...	
J. W. WHIT...	
C. E. WHIT...	
C. W. WHIT...	
C. WHIT...	
V. R. WHIT...	
U. L. WHITE...	
P. M. WHITL...	
E. H. WHITSON	

Name	Rank
W. B. WHITT	
A. T. WHITTEMORE	GM1c
E. M. WICK	MATT2c
J. J. WICKLUND	FC1c
A. A. WILCOX	S1c
J. W. WILL	QM1c
L. J. WILLETTE	S1c
A. D. WILLIAMS	S1c
C. R. WILLIAMS	MUS2c
G. W. WILLIAMS	S1c
J. H. WILLIAMS	S1c
L. "A" WILLIAMS	ENS
R. WILLIAMSON, Jr.	MATT1c
W. D. WILLIAMSON	RM2c
R. K. WILLIS, Jr.	S1c
B. M. WILSON	S1c
C. A. WILSON	S1c
H. W. WILSON	CBM
J. J. WILSON	F1c
N. M. WILSON	S1c
R. M. WILSON	CHMACH
P. E. WIMBERLEY	S1c
E. WINTER	GM1c
F. P. WOJTKIEWICZ	MACH
G. A. WOLF, Jr.	CMM
H. B. WOOD	ENS
H. V. WOOD	BM2c
R. E. WOOD	S1c
V. W. WOODS	F1c
A. A. WOODS	S1c
A. A. WOODWARD	MM1c
H. F. WOODY	S1c
N. B. WOOLF	S1c
E. H. WRIGHT	CWT
R. L. WYCKOFF	F1c
E. E. YATES	S1c
C. YEATS, Jr.	SC1c
F. P. YOMINE	COX
E. R. YOUNG	S1c
G. R. YOUNG	ENS
J. W. YOUNG	S1c
V. L. YOUNG	WT1c
J. V. ZEILER	S1c
...ZIEMBICKI	

Central inscription:

EMORY OF THE GALLANT MEN
OMBED AND THEIR SHIPMATES
E THEIR LIVES IN ACTION
BER 7, 1941 ON THE U.S.S. ARIZONA

THIS MEMORIAL WALL WAS INSTALLED AND REDEDICATED BY AMVETS NOVEMBER 2014

FOREWORD

BY DONALD STRATTON
USS Arizona *Survivor*

The USS *Arizona* was a very proud ship and my first assignment when I joined the U.S. Navy in 1940. I enjoyed my tour of duty aboard this beautiful ship, until it all came to an end on December 7, 1941.

I think my shipmates are glad the USS *Arizona* Memorial was built to honor the ship and its sacrifice. I know I am. For those of us who survived, as well as everyone from around the world, we can come aboard and look down to see the outline of the ship. We watch as the black drops of oil, called tears, float to the surface. But as this book illustrates, there is so much more to USS *Arizona* just below the surface.

When I look down from the Memorial, I remember all the hours spent on board, walking on those decks. I stand in the shrine room and pay respect to my shipmates, their names engraved in white marble. They are still serving our beautiful ship.

The impressive Memorial will continue to be visited by millions of people from all walks of life, young and old. They will continue to witness USS *Arizona*; they will remember all those who suffered on December 7, 1941. This book is an extension of that experience, to connect with our ship, to what is still there 75 years later, to understand its importance, both to the past and the future. And most of all, to pray it never happens again.

A final salute to all my shipmates,

Donald Stratton

August 2016

USS *Arizona* survivor Donald Stratton stands before the names of his fallen shipmates in the Memorial's Shrine Room in August 2016.

Previous: Visitors peer down at the ship through the viewing well on the Memorial.

How'd you like _Arizona_?

"I liked it very much. . . . of course . . . we had just gone aboard . . . and that thing was in dry dock with all the people hustling around and all the lines and welding lines and electrical cables and scraping the sides and the bottom and painting . . . I couldn't take six years of this, I don't think." (chuckles)

And was it different once you got to sea?

"Oh yes, quite different, you bet. And of course, everything squared itself away and everybody had their bunks and everybody had their general quarters stations, and everybody had their chow, where they had chow. And oh yes, it was very different and very good. I liked it."

Donald Stratton
USS Arizona _Survivor_

Dive operations on *Arizona* often take place after the departure of the last afternoon tourist boat to the Memorial, allowing NPS divers and researchers access to the Memorial during the evening hours. There is always something special about being part of a small group of passionate people working on *Arizona* when the sun fades and the national anthem plays over the loudspeakers during Evening Colors on the surrounding U.S. Navy base. If you are lucky enough to hear it, especially here, it's a chance to reflect about what a special place this is and what it means to be an American.

Page 13: Captain Charles Freeman escorts President Herbert Hoover during crew inspection on *Arizona*'s main deck. March 21, 1931.

Pages 14 - 15: *Arizona* underway in the East River heading to the New York Naval Yard after completing sea trials. The Brooklyn Bridge and Manhattan skyline is visible in the background. December 26, 1916.

IMAGING AN ICON

BY BRETT T. SEYMOUR
Deputy Chief, NPS Submerged Resources Center

In the spring of 1998, I received a phone call from Daniel Lenihan, then Chief of the National Park Service (NPS) Submerged Resources Center (SRC), inviting me to join a team from the SRC heading to Pearl Harbor. The goal of the project was to restore photo stations established by the NPS in the mid 1980s on USS *Arizona* that monitor the accumulation of marine encrustation. Kathy Billings, the new superintendent of the USS *Arizona* Memorial, believed underwater research was the key to understanding underwater sites. She also understood the importance of generating more imagery for the park's visitor education programs. I had no way of knowing that Daniel's call would spark a multidecade quest to image an icon.

Early in my NPS career, I never saw *Arizona* as a stranger. Although I had yet to visit Pearl Harbor, I had been exposed to hundreds of images in the slide files and the maps that decorated the walls of the SRC headquarters where I worked as a freelance photographer. I often heard Lenihan and former SRC Chief, Larry Murphy, speak of their work on *Arizona* with conviction. Now I would have the opportunity to experience what they both held to be the most significant dives of their careers. As I look back, many things have changed. I am now the Deputy Chief of the SRC and in my 20-plus years with the NPS, I have had the honor of diving on USS *Arizona* more than any other site.

My assignments with the SRC have ranged from photographing millennia-old shipwrecks to submerged World War II era aircraft and from the first Civil War submarine, *H.L. Hunley*, to the last immigrant ferryboat, *Ellis Island*.

NPS photographer Brett Seymour filming on the stern deck of the ship.

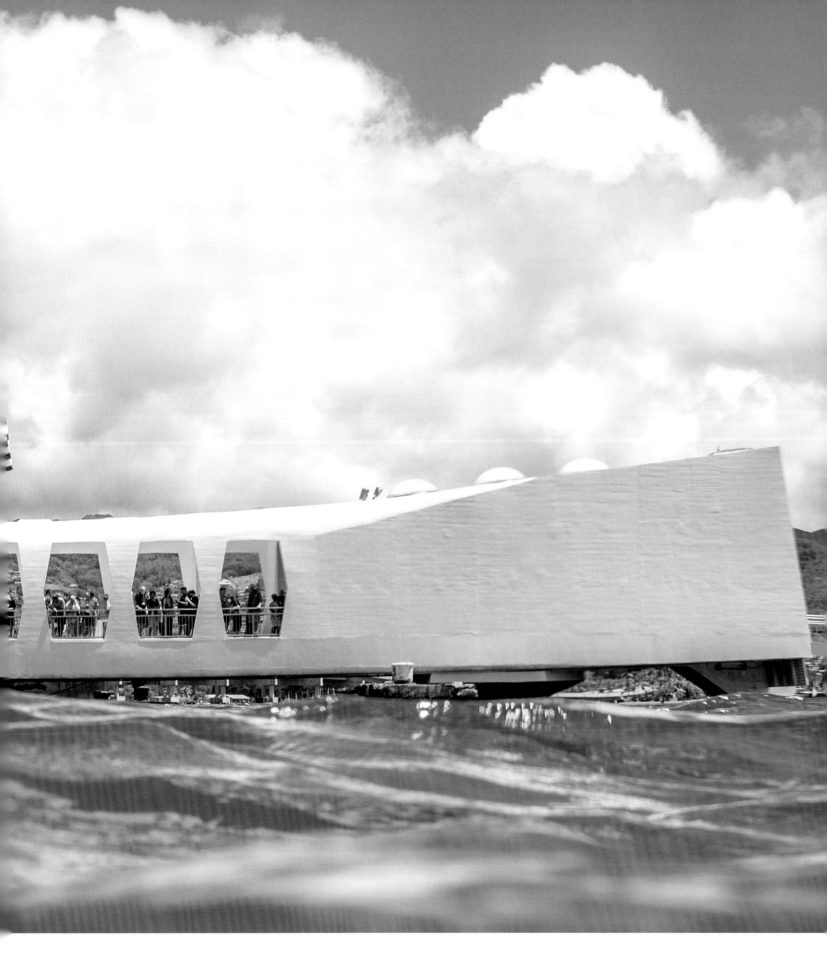

"On September 11, 2013, I had the privilege of escorting a unit of pararescue special forces on a tour of *Arizona* before they shipped out to the Middle East. For many it was not their first deployment. After the dive, the commanding officer turned to me and said, 'Thank you for what you do here.' I looked at him, stunned. 'Thank ME? I think you have it backward. Thank you and your men for what you do for all of us.' That dive marked my 300th dive on *Arizona*, a memorable dive indeed." - Brett Seymour

"... my single overriding goal has always been to create underwater imagery that reveals, inspires, and honors USS Arizona ..."

These sites all have heritage, but to me nothing compares with swimming the decks of USS *Arizona*. My dives on the ship have been diverse: tending remotely operated vehicles, being a human measuring-tape weight for SRC archeologists, supervising a Hollywood motion picture crew, and producing and shooting several large-scale documentary projects.

But rarely have I gotten wet without a camera. First armed only with 36 exposures on a film-based Nikonos V, I now dive with the latest megapixel-packed DSLR and 4K camera systems, which provide nearly unlimited images and instant gratification via an LCD monitor. With nearly 500 hours underwater on the ship, my single overriding goal has always been to create underwater imagery that reveals, inspires, and honors USS *Arizona* within the stewardship framework of the NPS.

As professional photographers go, I am somewhat of an anomaly. Most professional shooters, both on land and underwater, must constantly contend with copyright, stock agencies, and licensing. Protecting their work is difficult in this "save image as," social media-crazed, electronic world we live in. Although many I know are personally generous with their talents, often partnering with environmental organizations and nonprofits, they are still constrained by the demands of generating income and the cost of equipment or travel. As a professional photographer with the NPS, the images I generate are in the public domain. Simply put, they are available for all and I am unable to copyright them, therefore I can't profit from their sale. This allows my imagery on *Arizona* and other NPS sites to be shared freely. Equal parts access and ability have enabled me to create a

collection of photographs that educate and inspire those who will never scuba dive to see these sights firsthand—the very reason I became an underwater photographer.

The broken warship is both a dream and a nightmare assignment for an underwater shooter. The site is completely closed to any nonofficial diving. Even military diving is limited and closely monitored by the NPS. So, although 1,300 visitors a day view the site from above, the underwater realm of *Arizona* is tightly controlled. But that is where the advantages end. Trying to capture a 608-foot battleship in 3- to 6-foot visibility is a challenge. Obtaining the one image that tells the story is a quest—one I unknowingly began in 1998. For years I have been responding to well-meaning art directors or photo editors seeking a single shot that shows *Arizona* resting peacefully at the bottom of Pearl Harbor. I have dreamed of what that image might be for the past two decades. My typical recommendation is an *Arizona* painting by the talented Tom Freeman or the 3D digital model recently produced for the 75th anniversary. Neither is constrained by low visibility or air supply.

A watercolor painting by artist Tom Freeman based on the original 1984-86 NPS mapping operations, showing the remains of the broken battleship and the Memorial's position over the wreck. Reprinted with permission from Pacific Historic Parks.

Following: Sometimes on *Arizona*, the simple nature of artifacts can make a strong and lasting human connection. Here a collection of ceramic bowls rests in the sediment near the ship's galley (kitchen) where the men would have been gathered on the morning of December 7.

The two best images of my career have been given to me by *Arizona*—a career that has spanned perhaps hundreds of thousands of images. My favorite is on the opposite page, an image shot on film in the early 2000s. It was a morning dive with then Superintendent Kathy Billings and the visibility was outstanding, perhaps the best I have ever seen. The harbor was calm and the sun perfectly positioned behind the American flag, which gently swayed over the Memorial. For the first time I felt connected to the ship, not as a spectator but part of a story that began generations before me. Crouched in the galley area just below the Memorial looking up, I recall having a tremendous sense of peace and purpose as I framed a slight edge of the ship's galley gently illuminated by the sun passing through the white structure above. I held there, witnessing the reflection of over 1.8 million visitors a year, the inverse of their gaze onto the ship. I felt I had captured something special, but since it was film—one of only 36 frames available to me underwater—I had to agonizingly wait for processing. To this day, nearly 15 years later, that image is the only framed large print of my work hanging in my house, a wedding gift by my great friend and SRC colleague Matthew Russell with whom I had spent many amazing dives on *Arizona*.

My other favorite image was not the result of careful composition and limited exposures but just the opposite. While diving near the bow some years later, I noticed a torrential downpour overhead. I surfaced at the ship's bull nose, or edge of the bow, to witness an amazing collision of rain and harbor. A sea of gray was set against the white Memorial in the distance. Having the benefits of a digital camera, I began firing frame after frame, constantly dunking the camera housing briefly to clear the dome port of water drops and searching for a clean shot. The rain was violent, and the Memorial and all of Pearl Harbor felt completely vacant. I kept shooting, longing to capture the scene I had been privileged to witness. I shot until my memory card was full. The rain dissipated, the harbor brightened. My dive was over.

Sunlight streams through the Memorial highlighting an edge of the ship's galley.

" . . . for all those who sacrificed their lives; for those few who survived and asked why; for those who come to pay their respect; and perhaps, most importantly, for those who have yet to understand and connect."

Sometimes a moment translates in the camera, oftentimes not. When I was reviewing the images that evening, they all blurred together. Raindrops on the dome, the bend of water obscuring the Memorial, on and on they went. One image, one out of a hundred, maybe more, struck me. The dome was clear, the Memorial level, and the rain dancing off Pearl Harbor as I had experienced it. Did I capture the moment? As I examined the image closely, I noticed a single source of color in an otherwise gray landscape. Standing on the Memorial was a single visitor holding a yellow umbrella defying the falling downpour. I will never know who the individual was, but he or she unwillingly contributed to a striking image that captures the solemn nature of the Memorial, the way it individually affects those who visit.

I know somewhere on that ship is the next great photograph, and my quest to capture it has been the single, most rewarding aspect of my career. This book is largely an outpouring of that quest. A collection of images never before compiled, mine among others, that seeks to engage, enlighten, and most of all honor USS *Arizona*. It is for all those who sacrificed their lives; for those few who survived and asked why; for those who come to pay their respect; and perhaps, most importantly, for those who have yet to understand and connect. Year after year, the ship reveals a little bit more as I swim the decks, grateful for one more dive on *Arizona*. I honor the ship and those who call it theirs the best way I know how—with my camera.

A lone visitor stands on the Memorial during a rainstorm.

Following: NPS photographer Brett Seymour and volunteer diver Jim Koza ascending in the murky waters of Pearl Harbor with a custom 3D HD camera system built by the Advanced Imaging and Visualization Laboratory at Woods Hole Oceanographic Institution.

"... to me nothing compares with
swimming the decks of USS Arizona."

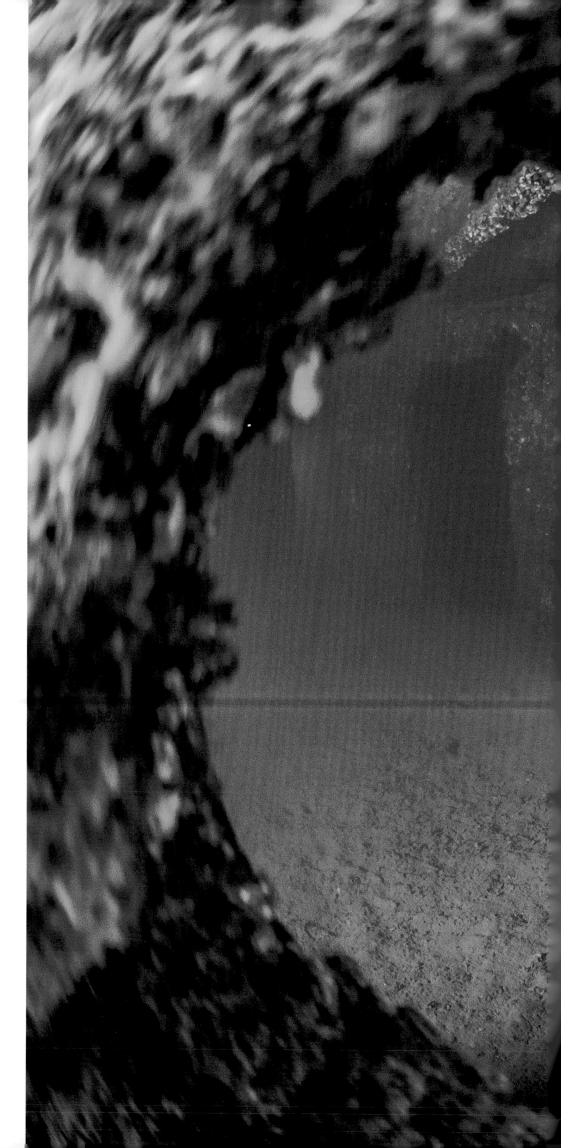

The view of the Division Marine
Office from an open porthole on
the starboard stern of the ship
reveals a nearly buried white
porcelain sink and writing desk. A
few open portholes allow interior
imaging of cabins on the second
deck by illuminating them with
high-powered lights through
adjacent portholes.

"I drove down and parked in front of the Officers' Club, Mary's Point Landing, that's where all the [rescue] boats came in from the ships. And I caught an Arizona boat I guess about ten, fifteen minutes after I arrived, and I think the second wave of the attack was taking place because they were strafing everything in sight. . . . I could see that Arizona had—something happened to Arizona because her berth was just covered with black smoke. And so the nearer we got to the Arizona berth, the more I could see that she was burning and just—you can't imagine the shock."

Everett Malcolm
USS Arizona *Survivor*

"I knew something had happened, so I ran over and I was looking down the carpenter's shop hatch when that torpedo that I had seen coming toward us must have went underneath . . . and hit the Arizona. . . . Arizona blew up from that torpedo . . . and it knocked me down and the flames were shooting over on our ship and everything . . . I just got up when the explosion, [the] force of it, knocked us [off the ship]. There was a bunch of us that blew out into the water. . . . the first thing I did was kick my shoes off and head for dry land."

Gene Huggins
USS Vestal *Survivor*

DIVING INTO HISTORY

33 Years of NPS Stewardship on USS *Arizona*

BY DANIEL J. LENIHAN

Former Chief, NPS Submerged Cultural Resources Unit

The USS *Arizona* rests heavy on the bottom of Pearl Harbor, weighed down by its own history. Seen from the walkway of the *Arizona* Memorial, its remains reveal little about what once was there. With the superstructure gone, random pieces of steel jutting from the water do not suggest a great warship. Nor do they hint that nearly a thousand men lie amidst the twisted bulkheads. Yet, visiting this place is a powerful experience for Americans. It's the idea of *Arizona* that people come to visit—not just a broken ship but everything it symbolizes—a time when Americans imagined themselves having been unified and strong.

We know 1,177 men died on the ship—more than half of all casualties from the December 7 attack. Nearly one thousand of them were unrecoverable, trapped inside the ship. An armor-piercing bomb penetrated the steel decks into the forward magazine, setting off hundreds of tons of explosives. For most of the crew, World War II was 10 minutes long—the Japanese planes attacked at 8:00 a.m. and USS *Arizona* was hit at 8:10. When a ship is ripped apart with such violence and burns for days, you don't try to count the dead. You add up survivors . . . then do a grim subtraction. The ones who lived swam through a sea of fire. They had life to celebrate only after years of recovery.

My first glimpse of *Arizona* underwater came in 1982 at the invitation of Gary Cummins, the Memorial superintendent. I was on my honeymoon and knew Gary had ulterior motives for serving as my rubber-finned tour guide as we snorkeled around the Memorial. When the park service took over managing the site in 1980,

NPS archeologist Daniel Lenihan at a porthole in the stern of the ship during mapping operations in 1986.

Previous: Battleship row, Pearl Harbor. December 7, 1941.

> **❝ With the superstructure gone, random pieces of steel jutting from the water do not suggest a great warship. Nor do they hint that nearly a thousand men lie amidst the twisted bulkheads. ❞**

Gary found himself steward of a major American shrine he couldn't see. He needed help. As chief of the park service team that provided such help to park managers (now the Submerged Resources Center [SRC]), I knew he wanted to show me, not tell me, the problem. It quickly became evident that Gary needed a detailed map of the ship's sunken hull and underwater imagery of its present condition. It sat in 40 feet of water with visibility ranging 5-7 feet over most of it.

There was little to go on. One would think if the Memorial straddled the ship, someone had to have mapped at least part of it. But the architect, Alfred Preis, neatly sidestepped that issue. The white Memorial spans the site without ever touching the ship—the builders needed only to know some places the ship wasn't, to sink pylons without hitting it. But Gary wanted to know exactly where it was, what it looked like, was it likely to collapse further, and where was that oil coming from? It seemed USS *Arizona* had successfully hidden under the feet of more than a million visitors a year.

A postcard we found in the National Park Service (NPS) visitor center proved helpful—a modern aerial perspective of *Arizona* with the Memorial. It gave a good sense of the hull outline, and gaping holes showed where the huge gun turrets had been salvaged and moved to shore batteries during the war. That was basically what we knew. The bombs caused a ½ kiloton explosion in the bow, and the base admirals warned it was very dangerous to dive. The lack of facts about what remained would be unthinkable if *Arizona* were on land.

The NPS had under its aegis, a submerged corroding battleship which had become a war grave held sacred by the American public. We suspected it still had in its bunkers a couple hundred thousand gallons of oil, which was slowly leaking out to form a thin but visible rainbow slick on the surface. The oil had become part of the *Arizona* experience—visitors saw the oil variably as blood or tears.

An aerial image of the USS *Arizona* Memorial with the remains of the sunken battleship visible beneath the surface of Pearl Harbor. A blue sheen of oil released from the ship can be seen at the top of the image.

It seemed USS Arizona had successfully hidden under the feet of more than a million visitors a year.

We knew no one had ever tried to map an object so large and complex underwater. Our team working the past two years at Isle Royale National Park in Lake Superior came closest in mapping large, comparatively recent ships. There, the challenges were depth and cold. Our methods, modified for low visibility, transferred reasonably well to Pearl Harbor. The warmth was welcome but the shallowness turned out to be a significant challenge. It was too shallow in the deck area for maneuvering and buoyancy control. I told Gary we would be there in 1983 for 10 days to scope out the job and come back in early 1984 to do it.

During our first day of diving in 1983, we swam right into the muzzles of the giant No. 1 guns that "weren't there." We found the guns and turret intact and in place. It couldn't be seen from aerial images because the forward deck collapsed deep into the hull, and light couldn't penetrate the murky water. We trial-tested a variation of our simple mapping techniques using string, measuring tapes, clothespins, geometry, and skilled diving illustrators.

By good fortune, just as we began operations, the dive industry found a way to replace the awkward black-and-white video systems we used. It had always been

The No. 1 gun turret.

Previous: A view of the Memorial from below.

> *During our first day of diving in 1983, we swam right into the muzzles of the giant No. 1 guns that 'weren't there.'*

necessary to send our video signal "topside." They could see what we were recording, but the diver couldn't. The operator was coached to pan up, left, move in, etc. But in 1983, a home-video craze began. The newly marketed, home-video cameras were a godsend for us. One arrived at our office in Santa Fe the day before I headed to Pearl Harbor. The 3" color monitor in the housing was the most exciting part. It may be hard for a nondiver to understand what it meant to see real-time what we filmed. We were self-contained—no cables necessary! On the first day, I recorded the newly found guns and our team's mapping operations. At the end of each workday, Gary handed a cassette to the local TV affiliates. The effect on Honolulu was electric. The second day we watched our work on the Hawaiian news go national, with a slow pan of the 14-inch guns.

The TV folks also showed pans of hatches looming open, porthole covers with trapped air from 1941, bomb holes, live ordnance, and personal artifacts—the tapes were a total surprise and grew more compelling each day. This vicarious return to the war by viewers was surpassed only by the intensity of each diver's experience. For all of them, park service and navy, they were undertaking a journey inside themselves as much as to the remains of *Arizona*. They were swimming through an iconic moment in their nation's history. Over 10 days, we learned what would be necessary in mapping a battleship, two football fields long in 5- to 7-foot visibility. We were ready to take on the main project in 1984.

My own memories of *Arizona* are tied to the abrasive feel of corrosion and heavy odor of seawater mixed with the unmistakable aftertaste of fuel oil. It was in our regulators, and you couldn't get it out of your hair each night. "Bunker C" fuel, standard for a ship of this period, oozed black ribbons along the overheads at a glacial pace until it could take off toward the surface in buoyant globules. At first, you had to hug the deck or any recognizable structure to not get lost.

We did not swim inside the wreck because *Arizona* is also a grave. Because of limited visibility, objects take form slowly as you swim toward them. They appear first as hints of a recognizable shape, then suddenly confirm or deny one's first impression.

A cluster of tiles dislodged from the floor of the ship's galley (kitchen) located below the Memorial.

Even mundane objects like shoes, medicine bottles, chain, and tile all become special in this place. Strafing holes in the deck are chilling signatures of death from above. Slivers of teak decking line the holes made by armor-piercing bombs. The bomb-entrance holes seem unreal. Did gravity really force them through multiple steel decks? These were just dropped from horizontal bombers, not dive bombers.

The sailors are with you all the time. Eventually, one's thoughts always return to them. I had one son and a second was on the way. Many of these men on *Arizona* couldn't legally buy a drink in most states.

The interaction of Japanese visitors with the veterans who volunteered as NPS guides always intrigued me. Some survivors embraced their former enemies while others turned away. For the latter, passing years have healed no wounds. Or maybe, they feel it's not their place to forgive their shipmates' killers—wounds borne now in peacetime yet never forgiven.

Two years later in 1986, subsequent Superintendent Bill Dickinson guided our next ventures to *Arizona*. He acknowledged that we had shown what was there but he wanted to know more. What would happen to it in the future?

Above: U.S. Navy Mobile Diving and Salvage Unit reserve divers from Long Beach, California, during NPS mapping operations in 1986.

Opposite: A drop of oil, often referred to as the "tears of the *Arizona*" by survivors, rises from a hatch near the ship's No. 4 barbette.

"*My own memories of Arizona are tied to the abrasive feel of corrosion and heavy odor of seawater mixed with the unmistakable aftertaste of fuel oil.*"

> **"** *The sailors are with you all the time.*
>   *Eventually, one's thoughts always return to them.* **"**

What about biofouling, specifics about corrosion, and exactly how much of the ship's oil was leaking? Most importantly, he thought we should do a comprehensive report on our Pearl Harbor work. Up until then, we had focused on specific questions, produced award-winning underwater maps, and wrote reports. Bill thought we should tell the whole story—how we did it, all the results collected from 1983 through his reign in 1988, and include our work on the *Utah,* a battleship converted to a target/training vessel sunk on the other side of Ford Island.

Our *Submerged Cultural Resources Study: USS* Arizona *and Pearl Harbor National Historic Landmark* came out in 1989 and has been a sales item for the park ever since. Much of its appeal came from the foldout line drawings of the 608-foot ship on the bottom. They were also assembled by Jerry Livingston, our chief illustrator, into a 5-part compilation that won the John Wesley Powell Award for Historic Display.

The project that started with my snorkel tour with Gary involved me intimately off and on with USS *Arizona* for a quarter century. We even carried down the ash-filled urns of survivors who passed away naturally. My last dives there were in 2011. The SRC's Brett Seymour developed a film project which was centered around me explaining underwater (through a face mask rigged for sound) how 28 years earlier we first documented the ship.

In 2016, the SRC regularly dives with the local NPS divers on *Arizona* and executes technical research and monitoring beyond what I ever imagined. Larry Murphy, my deputy who succeeded me as chief, wrote a series of scholarly journal reports with Matthew Russell and present chief, David Conlin. They projected in detail the effects of time, corrosion, and oil on the ship and the harbor that surrounds it.

The NPS also learned something as an agency from *Arizona*. It helped confirm how much it really needed a standing team of diving scientists to work in the unexpected underwater universe NPS cares for.

Located on the stern of *Arizona*, this open hatch with stairs once descended to the captain's cabin and stateroom on the second deck. Today it leads into 75 years of sediment buildup with only enough room for schooling fish to access the ship's interior.

Artifacts on the deck like
this glass bottle have been
inventoried, mapped, and tagged
as part of the NPS management
of the ship.

Following: A view from *Arizona*'s
bow looking aft at the 14-inch
guns of the No.1 and No. 2
turrets as the crew conducts
maintenance. Circa 1920.

"I was in the gun seat as a pointer, but the lights went out. We began to smell fumes of gas, of some type of poison from the batteries . . . below that the saltwater was getting into . . . all kinds of noises you could hear through the turret, believe it or not. And I decided that being in this turret wasn't the place for me. I needed to be on an anti-aircraft gun . . . the one my brother was on. I knew he had to be there. . . ."

John Anderson
USS Arizona *Survivor*

*USS *Arizona* had 38 sets of brothers on board the day of the attack on Pearl Harbor. John Anderson's twin brother, Delbert, did not survive. John rejoined his brother as the 41st crewmember interred in the ship on December 7, 2016—the 75th anniversary of the 1941 attack.

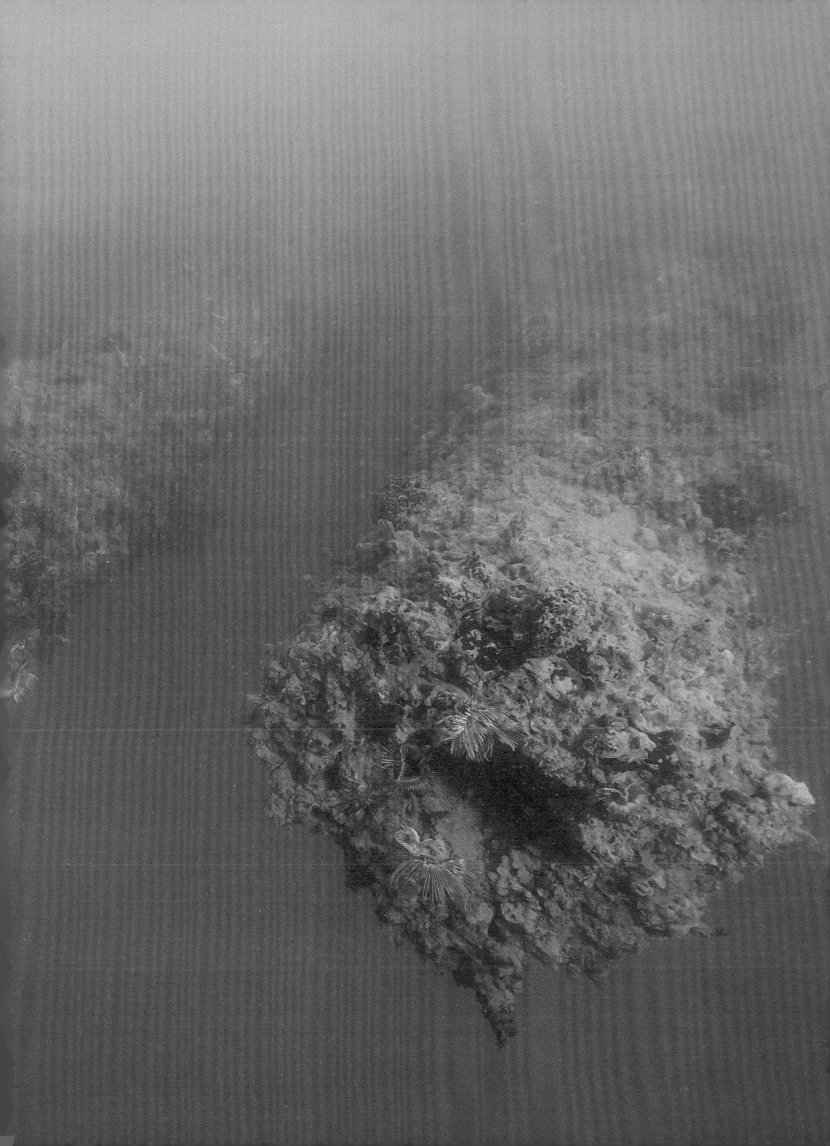

THE HISTORY OF REMEMBRANCE

DANIEL A. MARTINEZ

Chief Historian, World War II Valor in the Pacific National Monument

When I arrived in Hawaii in the summer of 1984, I was a seasonal ranger from Custer Battlefield National Monument in Montana. I had come to the USS *Arizona* Memorial for the purpose of working as a summer seasonal. During that first year, I met Michael Slackman, the park's historian, and enjoyed the pleasure of his company and historical expertise. I was taken by his passion for USS *Arizona* and his dedication to preserving the memory of Pearl Harbor.

On my first day of work, I went with Chief Ranger John Martini to the USS *Arizona* Memorial. For me, it was the first time I saw the dazzling white monument and the ghostly waters surrounding the wreckage of *Arizona*. It was an early morning, the waters were still, and a scent of oil drifted across this heroic landscape. Looking off to the stern section of the ship, I noticed a multicolored sheen of oil lazily floating by in majestic shapes and colors, twisted by the currents of Pearl Harbor.

I was emotionally and professionally hooked by the experience and decided my permanent career with the National Park Service (NPS) would begin here. Since both sides of my family were present on Oahu during the attack on December 7, 1941, it seemed especially fitting.

In 1983, just one year before I arrived, Superintendent Gary Cummins initiated the first mapping and photo-documentation of USS *Arizona* since 1943. He wanted to understand the current condition of the ship. Questions arose from Cummins' curiosity: Was the ship in imminent danger of falling apart? Where was the oil coming from?

An oily sheen over the wreckage mixes with an orchid thrown into Pearl Harbor by a visitor from the Memorial.

Previous: NOAA maritime archeologist and NPS volunteer diver Kelly Keogh illuminates the muzzles of *Arizona*'s No. 1 guns.

Did armament or live ordnance still exist in the wreckage? There was a flurry of historical and archeological questions posed by the superintendent and his staff. Clearly, understanding the condition of *Arizona* was riddled with contradiction and mystery.

Tasked with the job was the NPS Submerged Cultural Resources Unit (SCRU). A 10-day assessment was undertaken by the NPS and the U.S. Navy's Mobile Diving and Salvage Unit. The 1983 dives provided documentation to coordinate a comprehensive mapping project in 1984. For 21 days, drawings were produced in a mosaic pattern that documented 608 feet of hull and deck of *Arizona*. I was fortunate to be part of the topside team that gathered the drawings from the divers and brought them to NPS illustrator Jerry Livingston. As a historian, I was living the dream!

In 1986, underwater surveys of historic resources in Pearl Harbor were carried out by SCRU, which included an inspection of *Arizona*'s mooring quays and a search for Japanese aircraft wreckage. Dive operations were again underway at the site of USS *Arizona*, and for the first time at the USS *Utah*, the only two ships left in the harbor from the attack on December 7, 1941.

Above: Tagged artifacts from a sailor's shaving kit on the deck of *Arizona*.

Opposite: NPS archeologist Daniel Lenihan and NPS illustrator Jerry Livingston prepare for a dive on *Arizona* during the 1984 mapping operations.

Following: The 1894 *Arizona* illustration with handwritten notes from additional mapping dives in 1986, used as a reference for a physical model of the site.

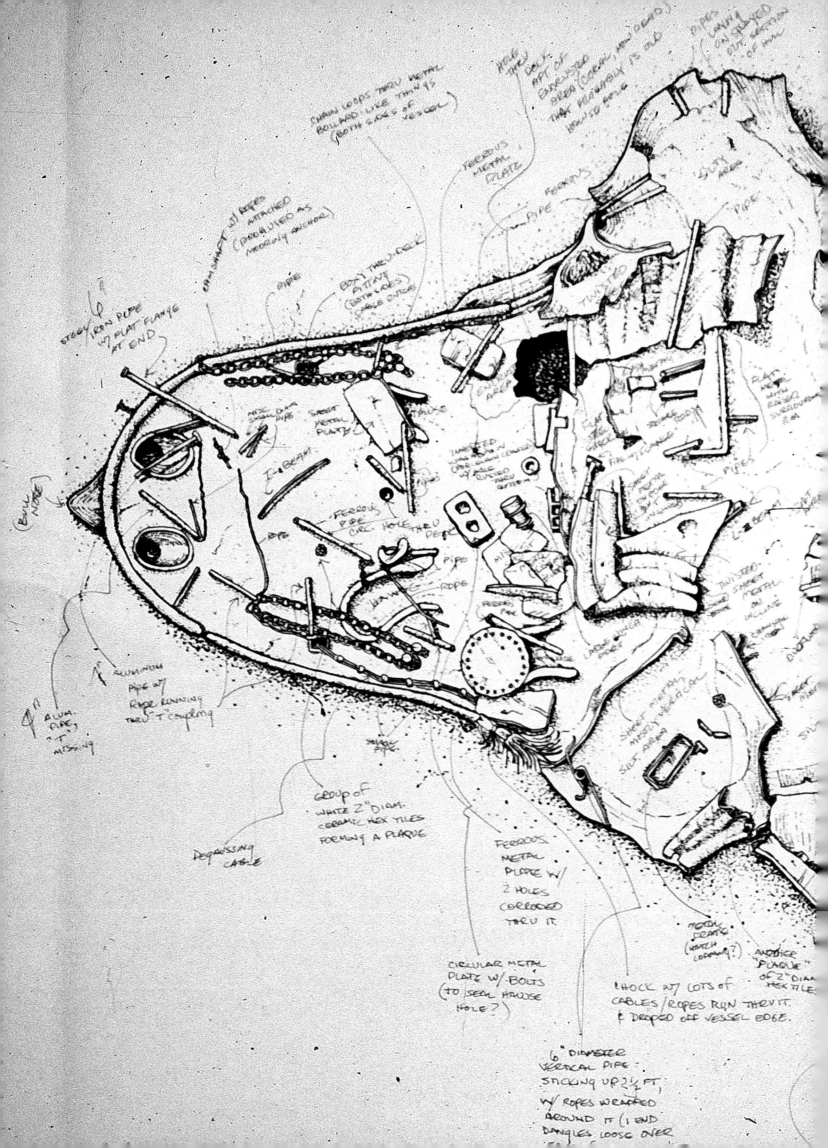

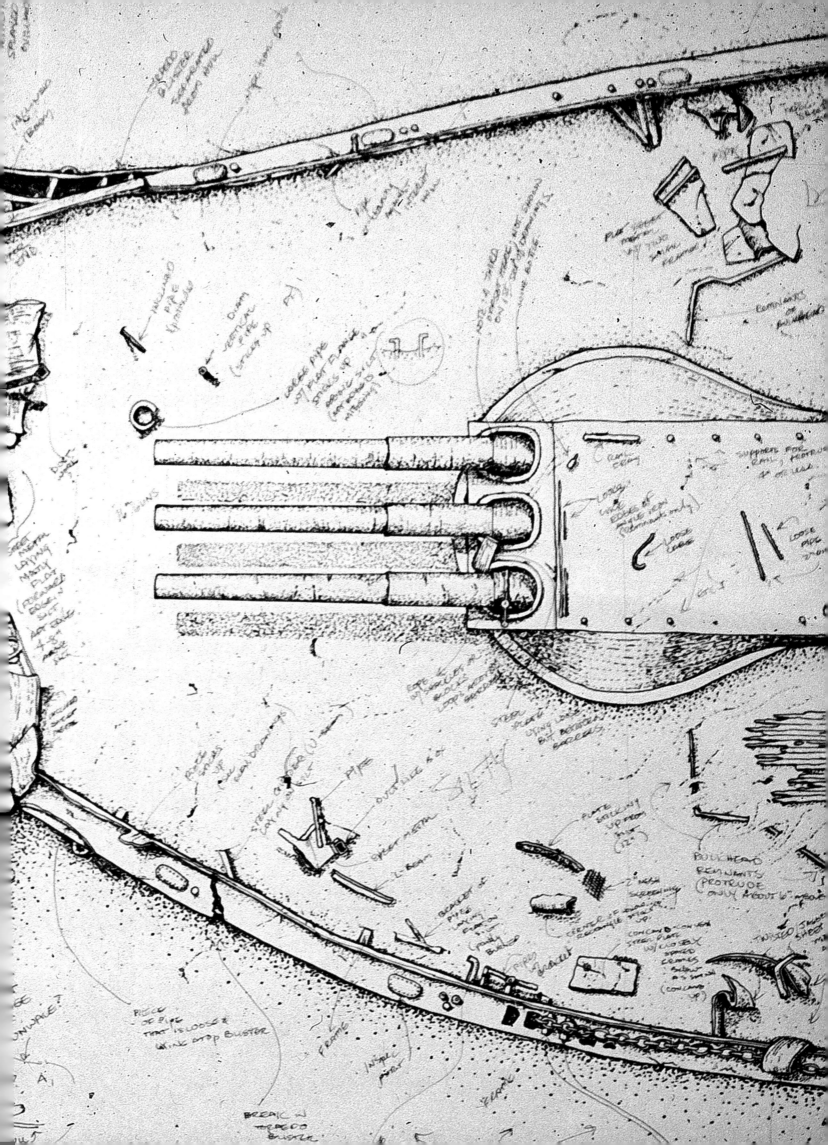

A wealth of information was derived from these scientific explorations. Drawings were done, photographs taken, and models made. A report, the *Submerged Cultural Resource Study*, was produced and published for professional and public interest and consumption.

The years leading up to the 50th anniversary of Pearl Harbor were fraught with controversy and political battles over the memory and commemoration of the Pacific War. This first national remembrance on December 7, 1991, was embodied in the icon of the USS *Arizona* Memorial. The image of the Memorial was ground zero for how we remembered that tragic day for America and Japan. The interpretive theme "From Engagement to Peace" resonates today for the visitors who come to the Pearl Harbor Visitor Center, although it is quite different from the time I arrived in 1984. But time has allowed us to move forward in recent years with the celebration of reconciliation and the recognition of this enduring legacy. A sense of peace and harmony now resonates at the site. Perhaps it is that premise we now embrace, thus ensuring the memory of the generation that fought in this horrific war is remembered, and the artifacts of the conflict will be preserved.

Above: Survivors from around the country gather each year to commemorate the events of Pearl Harbor.

Opposite: The flag flies at half-mast on September 11, 2013.

"*The image of the memorial was ground zero for how we remembered that tragic day for America and Japan.*"

A coiled fire hose on the ship's upper deck serves as a reminder of the futile efforts to fight the fires that engulfed *Arizona* and burned for nearly three days.

For decades after the construction of the Memorial, visitors often threw coins onto the deck of *Arizona* below. Today, despite occasional removal by the NPS, the ship's galley area and white hexagonal floor tiles are covered with thousands of coins from around the world.

Previous: (L) USS *Arizona* in dry dock, circa 1930. (R) NPS Volunteer-In-Park divers Lynn and Scott Taylor pause at the ship's bow, called the cutwater, after a web-based "Live Dive" in October 2015 commemorating the 100th anniversary of the ship's launching.

A SUPERINTENDENT'S PERSPECTIVE

BY KATHY BILLINGS
Former Superintendent, USS Arizona *Memorial*

During the almost seven years I worked at the USS *Arizona* Memorial, the ship USS *Arizona* came to mean many things to me.

It is a sacred war grave for most of the sailors who were killed on the ship on December 7, 1941. It is the physical memory of the sacrifices made by our countrymen and women at the beginning of World War II. It is the place where people come from around the world and reflect on the meaning of war, conflict, national and world politics, democracy, and liberty. The ship facilitates intense emotions and conversations that encompass the past and reflect on the future of our world. USS *Arizona* continues to leak oil, reminding us that our history is not forgotten, and we, as citizens, have a responsibility to honor, remember, and learn from our shared histories.

I was honored to be a steward of the ship. I felt a keen responsibility to protect it and honor the men who remain, as well as the survivors. Working as a park dive team member changed my perspective on the legacy of history. The physical condition of the ship exhibits the destruction of the attack; the oil leaking from *Arizona* is often interpreted as tears of the ship for those who died that day.

Through my dive experiences, I became closer to the story of the ship, the events of the day of the attack, and the survivors. I saw history through their memories. War became more real and emotional for me; it was not just history,

NPS Superintendent Kathy Billings photographs oil leaking from a hatch on the ship in 1999.

> **" War became more real and emotional for me; it was not just history, it was an experience I needed to learn from. History was not stuck in the past—we could and should learn from the past and not forget. "**

it was an experience I needed to learn from. History was not stuck in the past—we could and should learn from the past and not forget.

When I arrived at the USS *Arizona* Memorial, the initial mapping operations had already been completed, resulting in the *Submerged Cultural Resources Study*. The next step was moving a preservation plan forward. Working with the National Park Service (NPS) Submerged Resources Center (SRC)'s Daniel Lenihan, Larry Murphy, Brett Seymour, David Conlin, and Matthew Russell, we developed a plan to inventory the ship artifacts, analyze the condition of the ship's metal, measure the amount of oil remaining on the ship, and try to answer questions on what to do about the leaking oil. Studies done in partnership with University of Nebraska scientists on the metal corrosion rates and structural integrity of the ship can help guide future park managers and military leaders in planning for protection of the ship and the harbor.

My first dive on USS *Arizona* was with Jim Adams, the park dive officer. Jim wanted me to be able to understand what we, as stewards of the Memorial, were responsible for and invited me to join the park dive team. The NPS dives were conducted to monitor the ship's condition, inventory and check artifacts on the deck, and clean up trash that had ended up on the wreck. Entry inside the ship was not allowed. That first dive, the harbor water visibility was about 6 inches, and we could not see anything when we first jumped from the dock into the water. We swam to the ship and submerged adjacent to the Memorial. As a very small part of the ship came into view, jagged and ripped metal became evident. Small reef fish swam near us. Jim led me to the stern, crossing the opening of the No. 4 barbette where we could only see a few inches into the depths of it. Floating next to the ship on the starboard side, we could see the word *Arizona*, barely visible.

NPS archeologist Mathew Russell collects escaping oil for analysis. Through intensive research of biomarkers and the chemical degradation of the oil, the NPS was able to determine the difference between oil releasing from the ship that had been exposed to seawater for several months or years versus oil that was leaking directly from the oil bunkers below decks.

Following: Leaking oil from *Arizona* constantly creates a sheen on the surface of Pearl Harbor surrounding the ship. Here NOAA maritime archeologist and NPS volunteer diver Kelly Keogh surfaces just below the Memorial.

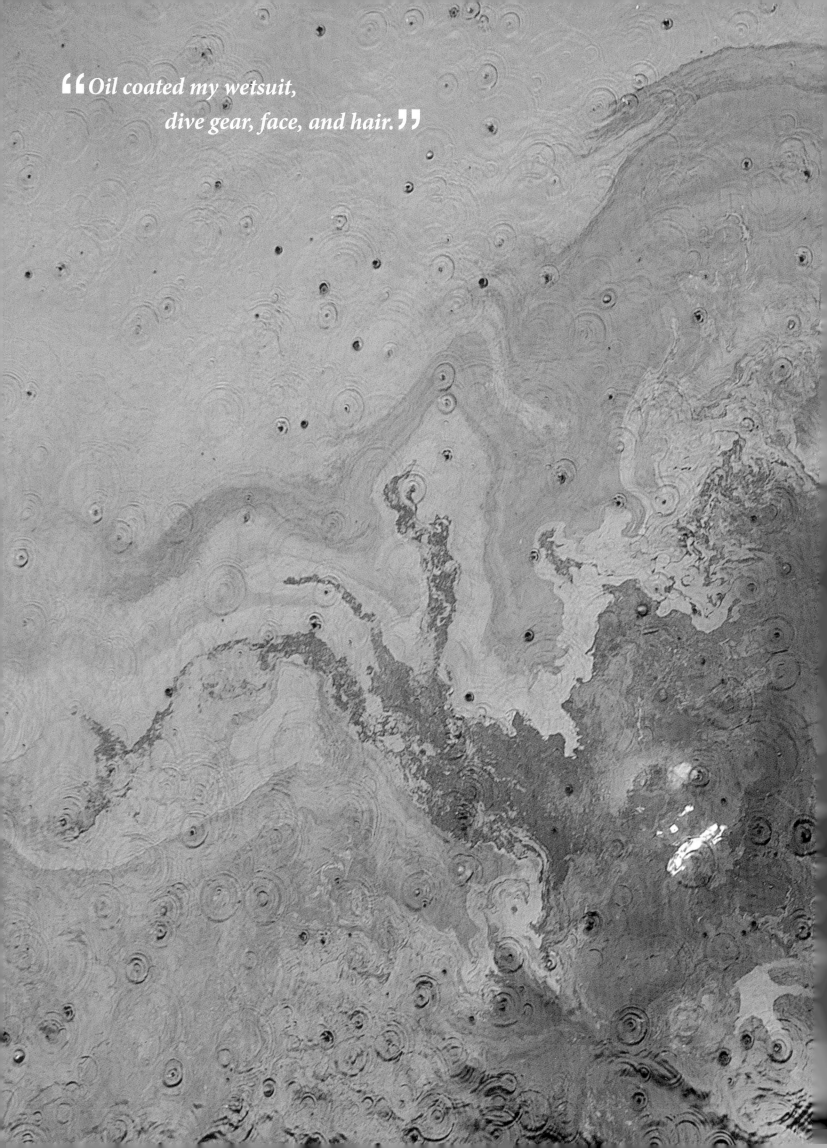

"Oil coated my wetsuit,
dive gear, face, and hair."

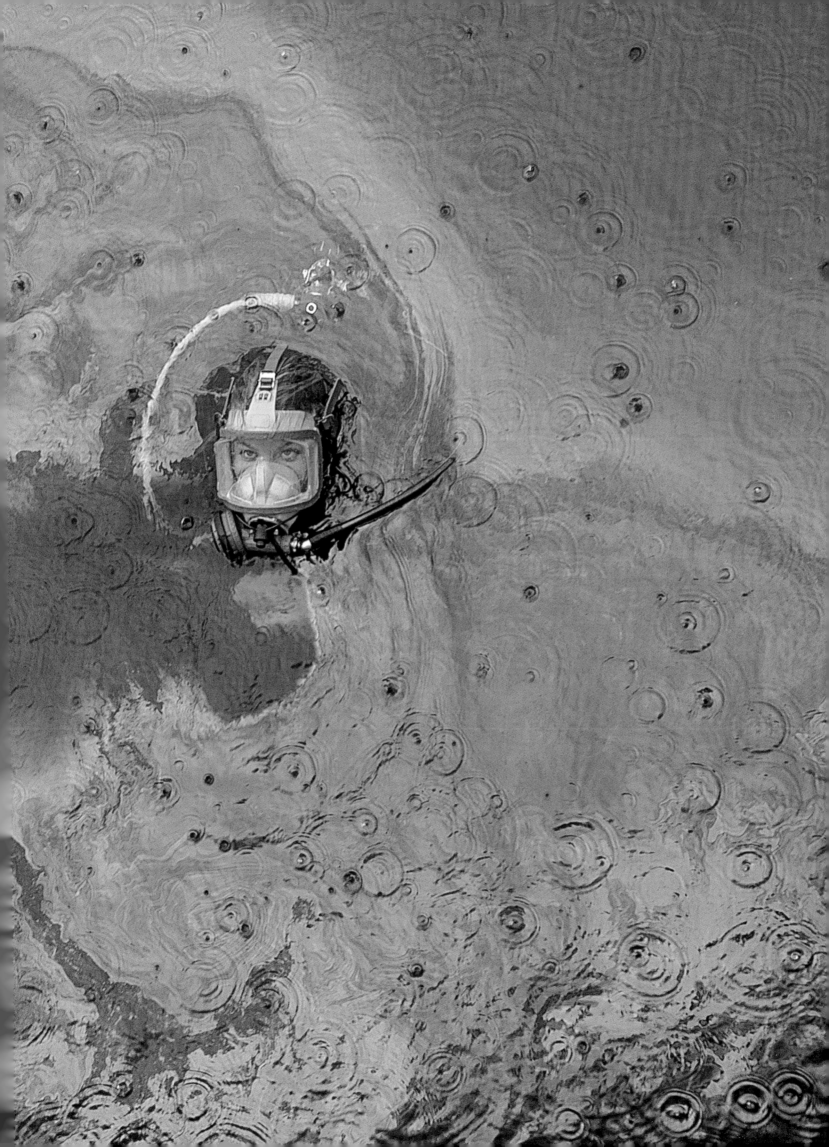

It was beautiful, eerie, and alive with marine growth. Oil coated my wetsuit, dive gear, face, and hair. The dive went to about 30 feet, where we unintentionally stirred up the very fine harbor silt creating zero visibility. We tried to find the No. 1 guns but missed them in the turbid water. It was an intense, emotional dive, unlike anything else I had ever experienced.

The first dive I completed with Daniel Lenihan was to the No. 1 guns. Daniel knew the ship, having mapped and recorded the locations and features in the years prior. Visibility was low that day, and we swam stern to bow, cutting from starboard to port. Suddenly, the front of the middle gun was directly in front of my mask. It was huge! We swam the length of the guns to the turret. The guns were still pointed to the mouth of Pearl Harbor, exactly where they were pointed on the day the ship sank. We swam to the bow, where the jumbled mass of metal bears witness to the powerful explosion that destroyed the ship. Seeing the guns and the bow close-up helped me understand in a small way the devastation that had occurred during the attack.

During an underwater archeological survey of the artifacts on the teak deck of the ship, I was assigned to hold the end of a measuring tape for one of the maritime archeologists. I had to stay in the same place for a half hour to an hour at a time. I was amazed to witness the diversity of life on the ship, including marine invertebrates, reef fish, turtles, and many types of marine plants. The ship had become a living reef and home for many types of marine life.

For the first four years of diving on the ship, the visibility was usually around 6 inches to one foot. It was difficult to see my dive buddy at most times, unless we were touching. The ship seemed extremely long as we swam from stern to bow. It was difficult to understand what I was seeing at first, but after numerous dives and studies of the submerged cultural resource map, it was easier to navigate to specific locations on the ship. The smell of leaking oil was ever-present on each dive. Around 1999-2000, Pearl Harbor's water became clearer. Diving visibility increased to over 10 feet.

Over the years as the Pearl Harbor environment improved, NPS divers began to notice an increase in marine species on the wreck. Sea turtles, schooling fish, spotted eagle rays, and the occasional seahorse are now frequently seen.

Following: NPS archeologist Bert Ho illuminates a 14-inch muzzle of *Arizona*'s No. 1 guns.

" The guns were still pointed to the mouth of Pearl Harbor, exactly where they were pointed on the day the ship sank. "

" *For many of them, their lives were defined by their ship, Pearl Harbor, and December 7. It was an honor for them to rejoin their shipmates.* **"**

It was easier to navigate and find locations during those dives, check on the condition of artifacts on the ship deck, and see the bow and the No. 1 guns.

During my tenure as superintendent, many USS *Arizona* survivors met with park staff and spoke of their desire to rejoin their shipmates when they passed away. For many of them, their lives were defined by their ship, Pearl Harbor, and December 7. It was an honor for them to rejoin their shipmates. We added the names of all of those interred to the marble benches in the Shrine Room so that their names joined those listed on the Shrine Room wall. The interment services with military honors were emotional for the families and the park staff. I was honored to participate as a diver during a survivor interment. It was one of the most affecting events I have ever experienced. Diving into the No. 4 barbette and placing the urn securely through an opening in the ship was a fulfillment of the survivor's request, a family's love, a rejoining of the survivor with his shipmates, and a legacy for all to remember the sacrifices of our military members.

Diving on USS *Arizona* was the most powerful experience I had of my entire career with the National Park Service. I was honored to have the privilege to be able to take care of the ship and its legacy and be a part of its research and protection. Diving with marine archeologists, scientists, filmmakers, photographers, and documentation teams provided a new understanding of the ship's condition and history of the Pearl Harbor attack.

The actual experience of diving on the ship is more than seeing photos. All of your senses are exposed to the past destruction of the ship. Respect and honor are integral to the experience, knowing you are diving around a war grave where many sailors remain forever.

USS *Arizona* survivor Ensign Joseph K. Langdell is interred inside the No. 4 barbette on December 7, 2015, by NPS volunteer diver Michael Freeman.

A small school of golden trevally swims across *Arizona*'s upper deck.

Previous: A dense coral colony grows on what once was a ventilation shaft midship, just below the Memorial.

Following: Brilliantly colored sea sponges carpet areas of the ship.

FIRST IMPRESSIONS

Life on USS *Arizona*

BY NAOMI S. BLINICK

Park Diver, World War II Valor in the Pacific National Monument

In 2011, I traveled to Pearl Harbor as an intern with the National Park Service (NPS) Submerged Resources Center (SRC). I was assisting Brett Seymour, the center's chief photographer, on a film shoot to capture underwater 3D footage of USS *Arizona* for education and outreach. I had no idea at the time that I would be back in Hawaii a few years later and would have the honor of serving on the park's dive team for two years. While there, I took part in additional photography and video work, coral research, site cleanups, and coordinating live underwater broadcasts by NPS divers on the ship.

I did my first dive on *Arizona* with Daniel Lenihan, the founder of the Submerged Cultural Resources Unit (predecessor to the SRC) and the driving force behind the documentation, mapping, and research on the site that began in 1982. Wearing full face masks with communication units, we descended into the murky harbor much to the curiosity of the Memorial's visitors. We swam from the floating dock toward the port quarter, and just as I thought we would never find the ship in the nearly opaque water, the outline of the gunwale materialized like an apparition.

I was told that the ship was covered in marine life, but I was still surprised to see the abundance of color that greeted me. Much of it peeked out from a thick blanket of sediment, but clearly life had reclaimed this relic of war and death. Sponges, corals, worms, and sea cucumbers—an incredibly vibrant array of filter- and sediment-feeding organisms—seemed to thrive here.

A sea cucumber (a bottom-dwelling marine invertebrate) on the stern main deck of *Arizona*.

Following: Abundant life blankets a partial wall remaining in *Arizona*'s galley.

> ❝ *We approached the No. 1 guns from the front, with the three massive muzzles pointing directly at us. Former symbols of military might, they now hosted encrusting marine life over every inch.* ❞

I later learned that a large number of the bottom-dwelling organisms growing on the wreck were not native to Hawaii but vestiges from the days when Pearl Harbor was home to the U.S. Navy's Pacific Fleet during World War II. At that time, ballast water was released in harbors without restriction, transporting life from port-to-port across the ocean. Many of these nonnative species represent the journey of the Pacific Fleet during wartime.

Being able to dive *Arizona* with Daniel was a real privilege. He continuously narrated as we circumnavigated the ship. Daniel examined how the condition of the wreck had changed since his last dives on the site, and I explored the eerie ship for the first time with his voice guiding me through the thick, dark water. As we swam along the hull, Daniel showed me the portholes through which the SRC sent remotely operated vehicles (ROVs) to document the interior of the ship. We swam along the deck and saw exposed areas of the original teak decking, the catapult base, and open hatches. Next we were in the shadow of the Memorial, which was over the ship's galley.

There were reminders of the breakfast traumatically disrupted on the morning of December 7: scattered dishes, a cooking pot, and sections of the galley's floor tiles still intact. The starboard hull up to the bow area was shattered by an explosion to the forward munitions compartment, and it seemed to be an indistinguishable mass of twisted metal. We approached the No. 1 guns from the front, with the three massive muzzles pointing directly at us. Former symbols of military might, they now host encrusting marine life over every inch.

To be on the site of such devastation and terror, a final resting place for so many lost lives, never ceases to put me in a state of introspection. Whenever I am

on the Memorial, and especially when diving in the murk below, I cannot help but think about the young sailors who fought for their lives on this exact spot, and how so many would never know the global resonance of what happened that day. They would never know the Japanese attack on Pearl Harbor didn't shatter the Pacific Fleet (as was hoped by its orchestrators) but solidified America's resolve to join the war, with failure being an unacceptable option. Nor would they know that the subsequent actions of American and other Allied troops would ultimately lead to my own grandparents' survival from the largest act of genocide committed in human history.

I am acutely aware that my own existence is due to the particular way events unfolded in the war and to the selfless sacrifices of so many. Caring for this resting place and helping share the story of that moment in history is what I can do to keep this story alive for future generations, and to honor the survivors and those who never made it off the ship.

NPS volunteer diver Naomi Blinick photographing the No. 1 guns.

Following: A stripebelly pufferfish peeks from under the ship's structure.

Sponges in a variety of pastel
shades cover *Arizona* as a living
reef.

Following: The stern gunwale
of *Arizona*, heavily coated in
sediment but still teeming with life.

"I was told the ship was covered in marine life, but I was still surprised to see the abundance of color that greeted me. Much of it peeked out from a thick blanket of sediment, but clearly life had reclaimed this relic of war and death."

Over the past two decades, *Arizona* has become a living reef amidst the once polluted waters of Pearl Harbor. Hard corals, schooling fish, and a variety of other organisms now call the ship home. Here a tiny crab hides among the coral polyps on a reef midship.

Following: The remains of *Arizona*'s No. 2 turret are visible from the surface at low tide.

Did you know how bad the *Arizona* was damaged, right away?

"Oh yes. . . . I knew she was . . . I knew they broke her back. I knew that."

Donald Stratton

USS Arizona *Survivor*

A SAILOR'S SERVICE

BY MICHAEL D. FREEMAN, CDR USN (RET)

Park Diver, World War II Valor in the Pacific National Monument

I served 22 years as a U.S. Navy surface warfare officer and deep sea diver, during which I commanded several navy salvage ships and diving units, deploying around the world. Upon retiring from the navy, I went back to sea as a merchant mariner. I returned to Pearl Harbor in September 2000 as a ship pilot.

My wife, Jeannie, was employed by the National Park Service (NPS) and transferred to the USS *Arizona* Memorial in 2001, working for Superintendent Kathy Billings. I could not believe my good fortune when Jeannie told me I might have a chance to help out the NPS as a diver in Pearl Harbor. Due to a diver shortage at the time and given my background as a navy diver, Kathy offered me the opportunity to become an NPS diver. I have been diving on USS *Arizona* and USS *Utah* for the past 15 years.

I completed my Blue Card qualifications (NPS diving certification) with Brett Seymour. Kathy then familiarized me with *Arizona, Utah*, and the various ongoing projects. With Kathy, everything was about respect for the sailors and marines entombed in the ship, supporting the Pearl Harbor survivors, and enhancing the visitors' experience. We picked up the various items that a million and a half visitors a year accidentally dropped in the water, gathered data for ongoing experiments and information requests, and worked with members of the Submerged Cultural Resources Unit (later renamed the Submerged Resources Center) when they were in town.

U.S. Navy ceremonial color guard lines the Memorial walkway during a USS *Arizona* survivor interment.

Previous: USS *Arizona* days after the December 7 attack. The ship's superstructure, visible in this photograph, was removed during the subsequent salvage operations.

“*As a U.S. Navy veteran, diving on USS Arizona means honoring those who have gone before me.*”

We also conducted interment ceremonies for those *Arizona*- and *Utah*-attack survivors who, upon their death, wished to join their shipmates entombed in the ship.

As a U.S. Navy veteran, diving on USS *Arizona* means honoring those who have gone before me. On each dive, I physically salute those sailors and marines entombed in the ship, imagine the life they lived on board, and ponder the similarities to my early shipboard career. Each artifact—the teak planks on deck, the 14-inch No. 1 guns, and the octagonal black-and-white tiles in the galley area—speak to me of the powerful warship so familiar to her crew.

Interment of survivors who wish to join their shipmates is always a memorable event. I am proud to honor the wishes of the sailor or marine and feel a special pride in talking to family members after the ceremony. The family must often make great sacrifices to honor the final wishes of the survivor, but I can tell they know they did the right thing after these beautiful, solemn ceremonies.

Above: NPS volunteer diver Michael Freeman holds the urn of USS *Arizona* survivor Joseph K. Langdell above the No. 4 barbette.

Opposite: This bronze plaque, mounted on a 27-ton lava rock on Ford Island in 1955 by the Navy Club of the United States of America, was the first memorial erected in honor of servicemen killed in the Pearl Harbor attack. Its presence inspired the creation of the present day USS *Arizona* Memorial.

Above: On December 7, 2014, four of the then nine remaining USS *Arizona* survivors—Lauren Bruner, John Anderson, Louis Conter, and Don Stratton—poured a "final toast" to their shipmates. The men raised original champagne glasses from USS *Arizona* with wine that was a gift to the survivors association from President Gerald Ford in 1975 as a symbol of the brotherhood and sacrifice on the day of the attack on Pearl Harbor.

Opposite: The "final toast" glass representing *Arizona*'s crew rests on the ship before being interred.

A poignant reminder of life aboard *Arizona*. This boot sole and heel were exposed in 2015 after sediment on the main deck was disturbed during tugboat operations in Pearl Harbor. Artifacts like this remind those who regularly dive *Arizona* of the human connection of the fallen battleship.

A LOOK INSIDE *ARIZONA*

BRETT T. SEYMOUR *Deputy Chief, NPS Submerged Resources Center*
EVAN J. KOVACS *Director of Underwater Photography, Advanced Imaging and Visualization Laboratory, Woods Hole Oceanographic Institution*

Because the wreck of *Arizona* is considered a war grave, long-standing National Park Service (NPS) policy prohibits divers from entering the interior of the ship itself. In addition, the sunken battleship is a dangerous place for even the most skilled diver. However, full study of the site requires some means of getting inside the ship to record its condition for comparative reference in future studies.

Remotely operated vehicles (ROVs) have revolutionized exploration of the underwater world because they can go where people cannot. They have become the "sharp end" of the exploration spear to scout ahead for unlimited numbers of hours before sending in dive teams for more specialized tasks. In many cases, ROVs are used in water too deep for divers to work in safely, but they are also used in shallow water where conditions are too cramped, too polluted, or too cold. They are also perfect for the wreck of *Arizona*, which may be structurally unstable and where researchers are intent on avoiding a human presence out of respect for the nearly one thousand entombed sailors and marines.

ROVs have been in existence for several decades, but they first caught the attention of the general public during the highly publicized exploration and penetration of the wreck of RMS *Titanic* more than 30 years ago. One of the stars of the 1985 *Titanic* documentation was *Jason Jr.*, a small ROV developed at Woods Hole Oceanographic Institution (WHOI) that demonstrated to a wide audience the utility of remote vehicle technology.

A prototype ROV descends to *Arizona.*

Previous: Although divers never enter *Arizona* out of respect for the sailors and marines entombed within, occasionally imagery can be captured through open portholes on the stern of the ship. Here the Division Marine Office on the ship's second deck is illuminated.

Jason Jr. was deployed from WHOI's legendary submarine *Alvin* and sent back pictures from deep inside the wreck. These photos captivated the imaginations of millions of people around the world and helped launch countless innovations for working in the deep sea.

Like most other technologies, ROVs have been made smaller, more capable, and less expensive over the last 30 years. The NPS Submerged Resources Center (SRC) began its interior investigation on USS *Arizona* in 2000 using a VideoRay, an early pioneer of the micro-inspection class ROV, in partnership with the National Geographic Society. This early generation VideoRay weighed about 8 pounds and was small enough to fit through *Arizona*'s open portholes on the stern and descend below decks via open hatches. The system was a standard definition video camera with a live feed via the tether, surrounded by thrusters for movement. During the expedition, the NPS gained valuable insight into the interior condition of *Arizona* despite only being able to access limited areas of the second and third decks in the ship's stern. Closed bulkheads or potential tether entanglements could have resulted in a loss of the ROV.

Above: NPS archeologist Bert Ho tends a prototype ROV with a custom tether spooling mechanism. This one-of-a-kind ROV is designed and built by the WHOI Advanced Imaging and Visualization Laboratory and Marine Imaging Technologies. It allows the vehicle to deploy tether as it travels inside the ship, minimizing drag and entanglement. Upon exit from the ship, the ROV retrieves its own tether.

Opposite: A conference table and overturned chair with exposed springs located in the sediment-filled Admiral's Cabin.

Remotely operated vehicles have revolutionized exploration of the underwater world because they can go where people cannot. They have become the 'sharp end' of the exploration spear . . .

The NPS helped prove the usefulness of micro ROVs during their initial exploration of the interior of USS *Arizona* more than 15 years ago. But since then, much has changed.

In 2016, as the 75th anniversary of Pearl Harbor approached, the NPS journeyed back into the interior with a slightly larger but more capable vehicle developed by WHOI and Marine Imaging Technologies (MITech). The vehicle carried stereoscopic 3D cameras that have more than 30 times the resolution of the earlier ROV and the ability to build 3D volumetric models that scientists can use to help calculate structural integrity of the wreck. The vehicle has a tether management system that deploys a fiber optic and copper tether from within the vehicle as opposed to pulling a tether down corridors, around corners, and down stairways, which is not only detrimental to the ship, but constantly hangs up the ROV. This feature alone allowed for increased range and ability within the wreck by disturbing less sediment, catching the tether less, and giving scientists greater capability for scientific instrumentation. Once again, pioneering technology has provided unprecedented access to the ship, enabling managers to continue to understand and plan for *Arizona*'s future.

Above: During a 2015 interior test of the WHOI/MITech ROV, this bed frame was imaged from an open porthole in the port stern of *Arizona.*

Opposite: Imaged by the WHOI/MITech ROV during a September 2016 interior investigation, this suit hangs silently in Wardroom Officers Stateroom BB on the third deck deep within *Arizona*'s stern. According to historical records, First Lieutenant John Paul Coursey of the U.S. Marine Corps, serving as Junior Marine Officer during the attack, occupied this cabin. Lt. Coursey survived the attack and went on to serve in the Philippines, Solomon Islands, Okinawa, and Palau during WWII.

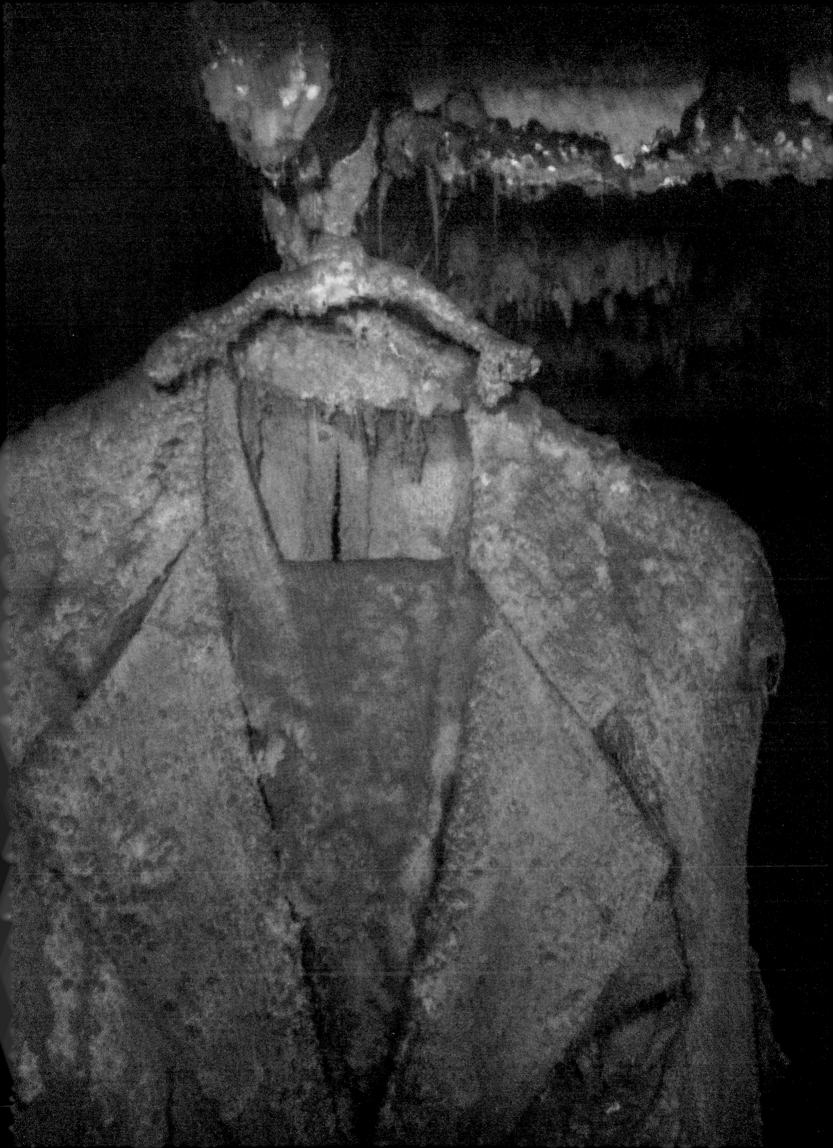

The prototype WHOI/MITech ROV investigates a sink and vanity in the Flag Section Stateroom on *Arizona*'s second deck.

"Once again, pioneering technology has provided unprecedented access to the ship, enabling managers to continue to understand and plan for Arizona's future."

"You know what a holystone is? . . . It's a brick about that big with a hole in it . . . they stick a broomstick in there and you get down and scrub these wood decks with it, to clean 'em . . . You get up at four o'clock in the morning to do this! . . . They swept and

then they washed 'em off with fire hoses and then you did the scrubbing . . . to make 'em white. They had to glisten. No oil spots, no gum . . . nothing better be on there when the captain came through . . ."

Ralph William Landreth
USS Arizona *Survivor*

Battleships are generally viewed as all iron or steel. Often overlooked is the warm wood that makes up the ship's main, or weather, deck. Occasionally, fish waft off the sediment to lay their eggs and expose the teak decking.

Previous: Crew sweeping the deck of USS *Arizona*.

BUILDING
CONNECTIONS

BY SCOTT R. PAWLOWSKI

*Chief of Cultural and Natural Resources, World War II Valor in
the Pacific National Monument*

So many friends, family, and visitors ask, "What is it like to work at the USS *Arizona*
Memorial?" You would think I'd have a good answer. For some people, this is just a
shorthand question about diving on the wreck. For others, it's a more nuanced question
about the gravity of the position and importance of decisions surrounding the ship.
The USS *Arizona* story is one of fellowship, devastation, memorialization, and remembrance that makes answering, "What's it like?" challenging. It's a question answered in
this book. These pages represent the best that we (World War II Valor in the Pacific National Monument and the Submerged Resources Center staff) have to share. If pictures
are worth a thousand words, they are surely worth many answers, too.

Battleships were cities gone to sea. Approximately 1,500 men lived on a ship that
measured 608 feet by 97 feet. In our museum collection, we have letters written home
from sailors talking about life aboard and how close fellow shipmates were to each
other. Even the ship's newspaper, *At'em* Arizona, regularly commented on crew cohe-
sion. Long before my arrival in Hawaii, park staff had been recording oral histories and
reminiscences from the crew. With more than 30 interviews (see www.nps.gov/valr),
these documents are a great read both on the events of December 7, 1941, and what
it was like to live aboard a U.S. Navy ship. Such fellowship still plays out today as the
survivors regularly keep in contact and stay abreast of each other's families. This is
one reason a cornerstone of our museum collection is about the soldiers and sailors
of USS *Arizona*. But we are losing these men and ideas to time. The men of *Arizona*!

NPS archeologist Matthew
Russell sets up a kinematic GPS
receiver on the ship's bow as part
of a multiyear research project
tracking any movement or
shifting of the vessel.

Following: Rays of sunlight
illuminate the ship's hull under
the Memorial.

"Devastation frequently imprints memories into our lives. USS Arizona was no exception."

Devastation frequently imprints memories into our lives. USS *Arizona* was no exception. On December 7, and for some time after, the ship's loss was one of the worst naval tragedies the United States had experienced. It was so terrible that the attack on Pearl Harbor and loss of USS *Arizona* galvanized a divided country to enter the war. The attack also led to a national holiday being created along with a memorial visited by over 1.8 million people annually. While we can watch the footage of the exploding ship or review images of USS *Arizona* burning at anchor, today there is very little tangible connection to those events. Visitors can only see small parts of the ship near the Memorial. This lack of easy connection has been why we have focused on photography, videography, and graphic visualizations. Our goal is to help visitors see and understand the twisted steel, splintered wood, and scattered artifacts in context of the physical destruction, loss of precious life, and subsequent events that changed history.

The question of memorialization is a complex issue. The simple questions of what, how, and why we memorialize quickly become difficult when you think about a multistakeholder interest group.

Above: The Memorial is suspended over *Arizona*'s hull, with the flagpole attached to the ship's original main mast. The rusting No. 3 barbette, or gun base, is one of the ship's few features visible to visitors.

Opposite: As part of the ongoing management of the site, NPS archeologists tag artifacts remaining on the exterior of *Arizona*. These .50-caliber rounds are remnants of an ammunition locker located in the forward part of the ship near the epicenter of the powder magazine explosion.

Following: NPS divers mapping the galley area of the ship.

"Our goal is to help visitors see and understand the twisted steel, splintered wood, and scattered artifacts in context of the physical destruction, loss of precious life, and subsequent events that changed history."

U.S.S. ARIZONA MEMORIAL 230

227 U.S.S. ARIZONA MEMORIAL

> **"** *It is here, in remembrance, that things get complicated, and it's what makes managing the USS Arizona Memorial such an honor and challenge.* **"**

Not all interests are aligned, and many may change over time. At Pearl Harbor, even Admirals Nimitz and Radford disagreed about the USS *Arizona* Memorial. Nimitz did not want to enshrine a bad day, while Radford thought about creating a beacon from which to learn. Today, diverse perspectives, balanced with realities of time, money, and resources, ensure our efforts to remember *Arizona* will continue to reach an ever-increasing number of people in the future.

Remembering what happened on December 7, 1941, might include easily understood emotions of sadness, thankfulness, and guilt. As a nation, we may feel guilty that we were unable to protect our citizens. But remembering can also be about inspiring, reification, and learning. We can build ourselves up by learning of the heroic acts that were displayed in difficult times. On a national scale, we also feel the deep rift left by the tragedy of losing so many vibrant citizens at once. Some people may want a marker cast in stone, concrete, or metal that displays the past visually. It is here, in remembrance, that things get complicated, and it's what makes managing the USS *Arizona* Memorial such an honor and challenge.

This challenging milieu is why, when during the design phase of the new Pearl Harbor Visitors Center Museum in 2007, Brett Seymour approached me with a proposal to create visual exhibits of USS *Arizona* today, I agreed. What was not to like? We were going to try to encapsulate the past visually with pictures or videos to give to future generations just by clicking a shutter or pushing a switch. Our journey to accomplish that task has taken us down some interesting new paths. Like a well laid-out garden, the initial goal of connecting with visitors seeded future work that grew into spectacular scientific research, photographs, ideas, 3D models and public engagement that continues today.

As part of the NPS's innovative management strategy, both the ship and some of the artifacts found on the decks have been digitally mapped utilizing photogrammetry, sonar, and laser technologies. In addition to 3D digital representations that will highlight changes to the ship over time, this digital mapping effort also produces tangible re-creations through the use of 3D printing. A Coca-Cola bottle located near the ship's galley (top image) has been reproduced as a 3D print (bottom image).

NPS archeologist Jessica Keller illuminates the stern of *Arizona*. It was here on the fantail with the deck slightly awash that the American flag still flew after the December 7 attack. Now, 75 years later, this area of the ship rests just 8 feet below the surface of Pearl Harbor.

Previous: The NPS has continually relied on external partnerships to both study and interpret *Arizona*. Here underwater cinematographer Pete Romano, ASC, owner of Hydroflex and longtime supporter of NPS underwater imaging projects, films with a digital cinema camera used for Hollywood motion pictures.

THE SCIENCE OF STEWARDSHIP

MATTHEW A. RUSSELL *Archeologist, NPS Submerged Resources Center*
LARRY E. MURPHY *Former Chief, NPS Submerged Resources Center*
DAVID L. CONLIN *Chief, NPS Submerged Resources Center*

One of our nation's most hallowed war graves, *Arizona*, is slowly disintegrating after a lifespan of 100 years and exactly 75 years half buried in the muddy bottom of Pearl Harbor. In addition to preserving this national icon for future generations, the National Park Service (NPS) also actively gathers scientific data to contribute to the environmental management of the site. Along with remains of nearly 1,000 sailors and marines, this scene of terrible tragedy and sacrifice still contains an estimated half-million gallons of fuel oil inside a deteriorating hull. As the battleship gradually collapses, the oil's release is inevitable. Simple questions such as, "How long do we have until the ship loses its integrity?" and "Is there anything we can do to delay this deterioration?" lead to complex answers with a dizzying number of variables, many of which we don't fully understand and perhaps a few of which we have overlooked completely.

To provide complex scientific answers to simple questions about the ship's future, our team from the NPS Submerged Resources Center with our partners from World War II Valor in the Pacific National Monument and others in the public and private sectors have undertaken an ambitious research program to develop a long-term preservation plan for the ship. The primary focus of our research is aimed at determining the nature and rate of corrosion attacking the ship's hull. One way to understand the overall corrosion process is by analyzing data from scientific measurements taken systematically along the hull, now mostly submerged. These measurements help engineers and other scientists understand past, current, and possible future hull corrosion.

NPS archeologist Matthew Russell uses a Cygnus gauge in an attempt to measure the thickness of *Arizona*'s hull. Despite several attempts, the ultrasonic thickness gauge was never successful in accurately or repeatedly measuring the thickness of the steel.

Following: NPS GPS coordinator Tim Smith establishes a precise 3D position with a geodetic GPS receiver on the deck of *Arizona* during a survey to monitor any movement of *Arizona*'s hull.

   " *The ship is not an empty shell, with corrosion happening only on visible surfaces—it is a complex three-dimensional structure with a maze of interior passageways and bulkheads that contribute to overall hull strength.* **"**

Characterizing hull corrosion has a profound effect on our understanding of remaining and future structural integrity.

At selected hull locations, NPS archeologists and University of Nebraska metallurgists examine and sample the scab of living and dead marine organisms and corrosion by-products that cover the vessel's exposed steel remains. This concretion holds secrets about what's going on with the remaining metal of the ship's hull.

With a pneumatic drill, we bore through this encrustation (which is usually about a ½" thick) and at selected intervals, insert a small probe to measure the microscopic environment that lies beneath the scab. Within this tiny sandwiched space between the concretion and the remaining hull, strange and unexpected microenvironments exist that we did not expect but contribute significantly to the preservation and deterioration of the ship.

Data about pH (acidity) and corrosion potential, a direct measure of the steel hull's active corrosion at that spot, give us some insight into what is happening on and to this iconic structure. We did this over many transects, from bow to stern, port and starboard, from the upper deck to below the point where the hull disappears into the mud—dozens of data sample locations and thousands of individual measurements. Data from these measurements are plotted, analyzed, and compared to get a better idea of how the ship is corroding, and if corrosion is uniform along the exposed hull.

Another important part of studying *Arizona*'s corrosion is investigating what is happening inside the ship. The ship is not an empty shell, with corrosion happening only on visible surfaces—it is a complex three-dimensional structure with a maze of interior passageways and bulkheads that contribute to overall hull strength. Consequently, we must understand interior corrosion as well as the more easily measured exterior hull corrosion. Although we are keenly aware of the sensitivity about entering a war grave, collecting interior data is crucial to developing a realistic model of the ship's deterioration. Out of respect for our fallen and also the ever-present danger posed to divers entering the vessel, we investigate interior spaces only with remotely operated technology.

NPS archeologist David Conlin lowers a WHOI engineered ROV with a 3D camera system into *Arizona* for survey.

Following: Artifacts lie on *Arizona*'s decks over the entire 608-foot length of the ship. Many have been blunted by 75 years underwater with marine growth. In the ship's galley area there is no mistaking the shape of this cooking pot, perhaps discarded after the blast or overlooked during the ship's salvage activities.

Using a miniature remotely operated vehicle (ROV), we search for access to the ship's lower decks where the fuel bunkers are located and gather crucial data on interior corrosion rates. Along the way, we bring back many remarkable images from deep inside the ship. Our small ROV is about the size of a toaster, so we easily deploy it into various hatches and openings in the hull. Sitting in the control room on the Memorial above, we navigate the ROV along corroding passageways and down crumbling stairways to points deep inside the battleship, where we collect a variety of scientific data that relates to corrosion, deterioration, and preservation, such as dissolved oxygen levels, pH, temperature, and salinity, with the ROV's onboard instruments. These parameters directly influence steel corrosion in seawater and allow us to compare interior deterioration rates to those on the outside. We also measure bulkhead thickness using an ultrasonic thickness gauge and collect samples of concretion, sediment, water, and oil from inside the ship for later analysis.

The next step is to bring together the data we collected into some scientifically useful form to help shape the tough decisions the NPS and U.S. Navy managers make about *Arizona* and the oil within the ship. Complex computer modeling, known as a finite element analysis, is used to collate all the data to predict the sequence of the battleship's deterioration and give managers an idea of how long we have before significant hull deterioration occurs and oil is released.

The NPS teamed with metallurgists and engineers from the National Institute of Standards and Technology (NIST) in Gaithersburg, Maryland, to conduct this analysis. These NIST scientists brought experience and techniques used for analysis of RMS *Titanic* and the steel from the World Trade Center. They reconstructed USS *Arizona* digitally in a powerful software package, starting with the ship as built on the day of the attack, then added the effects of the fatal blast and 75 years of immersion in saltwater to bring it up to the present. Next, using data collected on the battleship's corrosion rate both inside and out, they projected the model into the future to see how quickly and in what way the ship was likely to disintegrate.

A member of the U.S. Navy's Mobile Diving and Salvage Unit #1 operates a pneumatic drill press on *Arizona*'s hull to remove coupons, or samples, which help NPS researchers measure the rate of deterioration and structural integrity of the battleship.

NPS archeologist Jessica Keller shoots a series of photographs to create a 360 degree view from the ship's steam catapult base, located on the stern of *Arizona*.

This analysis is ongoing, but the data allows us to explore ways to slow the corrosion process. It ensures the ship's preservation for future generations as an icon to sacrifice, a touchstone to an era, and a generation that is slipping away much too fast.

Inevitably, we come back to the question of oil removal: Should preservation of a hallowed naval tomb take precedence over the active prevention of a large, potentially catastrophic oil spill of the ship's remaining fuel? The U.S. Navy and several commercial firms have the technical know-how and capability to empty sunken ships of their environmentally unfriendly fluids. Yet, this is USS *Arizona* in Pearl Harbor, and other factors besides straightforward oil removal need to be considered. For example, oil removal would be a very destructive procedure. *Arizona*'s hundreds of individual fuel oil bunkers are spread across three deck levels and the ship's double bottom. They are dispersed from bow to stern and port to starboard. The bunkers are highly compartmentalized, designed to prevent catastrophic fuel loss should one part of the battleship suffer a blow during combat.

As part of the digital mapping operations, an underwater laser, known as lidar, was deployed on the ship's stern to generate high-resolution point clouds of certain features.

> **" Our decisions need to be based on sound, scientific evidence, not preconceived notions or gut reactions. "**

Further complicating matters, all the fuel oil storage bunkers are beneath the present harbor bottom. The ship has sunk into the sediment of Pearl Harbor to almost exactly its original waterline, making direct access to the bunkers impossible.

Is this invasive and damaging procedure appropriate or acceptable on this hallowed site? Most authorities, including the NPS, think not, at least not without considerably more information about the impact to the ship as a whole and the remains of its crew specifically. In addition to its symbolic and historical importance, *Arizona* also was designated a National Historic Landmark in 1989, the highest level of significance bestowed by our country to beloved structures and symbols of our past. This means out of our obligation to the sailors and marines that still lie within this massive sepulture, and out of an obligation to generations yet to come, we need to move carefully and thoughtfully before proceeding with any intrusive or irreversible action. Our decisions need to be based on sound, scientific evidence, not preconceived notions or gut reactions.

As stewards of this remarkable, tragic, yet inspiring site, the NPS is working with its many partnering scientists and the U.S. Navy to determine the best course of action. In the meantime, our efforts are directed at discovering how long we have to make a decision and what possible options we have to slow the deterioration process so that managers can study and make the most informed decisions possible. So far, we have learned that we have some time to plan and be proactive; time to come up with the most-efficient, least-intrusive, and best course of action for USS *Arizona* as well as the other naval grave in Pearl Harbor—USS *Utah*. These historic vessels deserve nothing less than our very best efforts, best thinking, and best science.

Following: An air pocket from December 1941 still remains trapped between the glass porthole and an interior blast cover on *Arizona*'s main deck.

Pages 158-159: NPS archeologist Bert Ho illuminates a hatch with its awning still intact between *Arizona*'s No. 1 and 2 turrets. This hatch once led to the ship's carpenter shop, dental office, and sick bay. Those areas are now inaccessible. The fatal ignition of the forward powder magazine by an aerial bomb resulted in the total collapse of three decks and ultimate destruction of ship.

How do you visualize the *Arizona* when you think of her?

"By the big picture I['ve] got in my den. At sea, steaming."

Alive.

"Yeah. I think she'll always be, to me, she'll be alive. . . . she's a memorial . . ."

In your mind . . .

"In my mind, she lives."

John H. McCarron
USS **Arizona** *Survivor*

Acknowledgments

I would like to thank the National Park Service, an agency, culture, and individuals that I believe in, and have dedicated the first 20 years of my career striving to enhance its mission and mandate. To the NPS Submerged Resources Center (and SCRU), an organization and ethos I embraced before I even knew what a career was and never let go. To Daniel Lenihan, my mentor, confidant, and friend who took a chance on a budding film school grad decades ago, then backed me for years following. I will always be grateful.

I would like to thank the current and past staff of USS *Arizona* Memorial / World War II Valor in the Pacific National Monument for putting up with "the dive team" over the years as we sought to enhance, engage, and understand *Arizona* on your behalf. To Kathy Billings, thank you for funding a tiny contract to organize your video and slide files which first brought me to Pearl Harbor. Unknowingly you sparked a passion to photograph the broken battleship that is very much alive today. Thank you to my colleague, friend, and coauthor Naomi Blinick for your hard work helping me take an idea and turning it into a publication that reflects a passion for USS *Arizona*.

Lastly, I would like to thank the crew of USS *Arizona* itself, those who gave their lives on that day of infamy and those whose voices have faded since. I have had the privilege of both knowing some and laying others to rest inside the ship. They have all been remarkable men in my eyes. Not only for what they experienced, but how they went on to serve . . . and to live. To Don Stratton and his family, thank you for your friendship and willingness to help the Park Service at every turn as we seek to honor your ship and never forget.

Brett Seymour
September 11, 2016

To my coauthor Brett Seymour, you are mentorship defined. Thank you for giving me my first opportunities with an underwater camera and for your unwavering confidence in me. I am so honored to have been a part of this work with you.

An enormous thank you to the entire team at World War II Valor in the Pacific National Monument, who made me feel welcome from my first day at the park. In particular, I am so grateful to Scott Pawlowski for his tireless efforts to help me find my place in the ever-changing landscape and getting me in the water as much as possible.

To the crew of the Submerged Resources Center, especially David Conlin, who have consistently gone above and beyond in their support and friendship. Without your guidance and trust, I cannot say where I would be today. My first trip to Pearl Harbor has led me to places I never could have imagined, thanks to you.

To the lost and to the survivors, for the role you played in the shaping of history, I cannot extend enough of an honor. I am humbled to share in this homage to your sacrifice.

Naomi Blinick
September 11, 2016

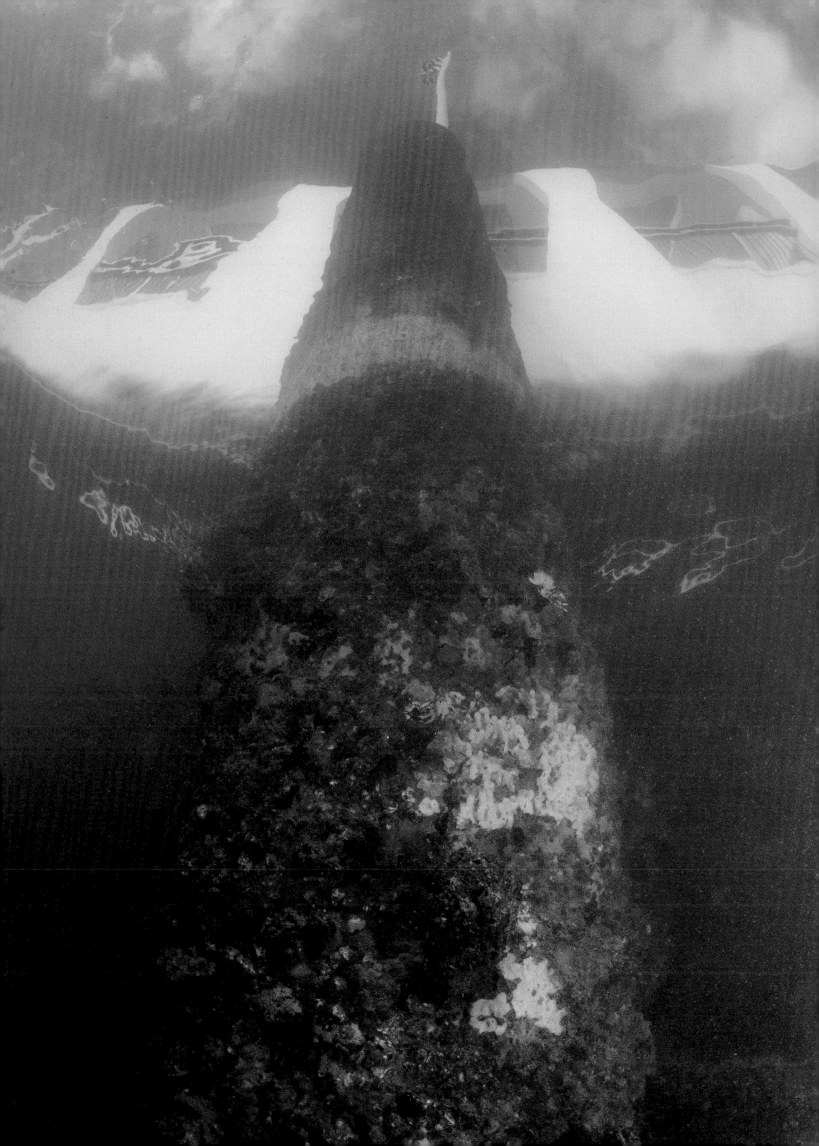

An NPS Honor Guard stands at attention in the Memorial Shrine Room during the 69th commemoration events on December 7, 2010.

Previous: USS *Arizona*'s mainmast where the American flag once flew, as seen from underwater on the ship's main deck. The current flag flies from a new pole attached to the original mainmast, representing the only physical connection the Memorial has with the ship.

Following: USS *Arizona* Memorial at dusk.

About the Authors

Brett Seymour is the Deputy Chief of the U.S. National Park Service's (NPS) Submerged Resources Center (SRC) based in Denver, Colorado. Formally known as the Submerged Cultural Resources Unit (or SCRU team), the SRC supports stewardship for the protection, preservation, public access, and interpretation of submerged resources, both in the United States and internationally.

Brett has been working as a full-time underwater photographer with the NPS since 1994. His work with the Service has provided underwater access to some of the United States most captivating national parks. In addition to making a whole new dimension of the Park system available to the public, for the past two decades, Brett has specialized in documenting historically significant underwater sites around the world.

More about the NPS Submerged Resources Center can be found at www.nps.gov/src. Brett's photographic work documenting the NPS's underwater realm (among other expeditions) can be found at www.brettseymourphotography.com.

Naomi Blinick is a freelance photographer and marine biologist. She has worked with the National Park Service's Submerged Resources Center in varying capacities since 2011. While living in Hawaii from 2014-2015, she was affiliated with World War II Valor in the Pacific National Monument, both as a volunteer diver and as a multimedia specialist for the park. During that time, she assisted with several media and scientific projects, including 3D mapping, coral recruitment research, and live underwater broadcasts. At the time of writing she is based in Cape Cod, MA.

Her photographs from Pearl Harbor and other National Park units can be found at www.naomiblinick.com.

Image Credits

All photographs taken by Brett Seymour, NPS, with the exception of:

13 World War II Valor in the Pacific NM Archives; 14 World War II Valor in the Pacific NM Archives; 18 Naomi Blinick, NPS; 23 Tom Freeman (reprinted with permission from Pacific Historic Parks); 30 Naomi Blinick, NPS; 35 World War II Valor in the Pacific NM Archives; 36 NPS Submerged Resources Center archives; 39 NPS Photo; 40 David Conlin, NPS; 46 NPS Submerged Resources Center archives; 50 NPS Photo; 53 World War II Valor in the Pacific NM Archives; 60 NPS Submerged Resources Center archives; 66 World War II Valor in the Pacific NM Archives; 88 Naomi Blinick, NPS; 90 Naomi Blinick, NPS; 98 Naomi Blinick, NPS; 104 World War II Valor in the Pacific NM Archives; 106 NPS Photo; 108 Susanna Pershern, NPS; 110 Shaan Hurley; 121 NPS SRC/WHOI/MITech ROV image; 124 World War II Valor in the Pacific NM Archives; 130 Jessica Keller, NPS; 137 Naomi Blinick, NPS; 161 World War II Valor in the Pacific NM Archives; 164 Susanna Pershern, NPS; 168 Elyse Butler (top image).